Television and College Students

Television and College Students

Surojit Sen Gupta

AKANSHA PUBLISHING HOUSE
NEW DELHI • GUWAHATI • VISAKHAPATNAM

AKANSHA PUBLISHING HOUSE
4649-B/21, Ansari Road
Darya Ganj, New Delhi - 110 002
Ph.: 23263193 / 9811582579 / 09435116718
Fax: 011-23263193
Email: ektabooks@yahoo.com
www.akanshapublishinghouse.com

Television and College Students

First Published 2010
ISBN 978-81-8370-250-8

PRINTED IN INDIA

Published by Akansha Publishing House, New Delhi and Printed at Harmain Offset Press, Delhi.

This book is a humble offering in the loving memory of my beloved father, Late Arunendu Selchar Sen Gupta.

Contents

Foreword

Television is the most pervasive, exciting and powerful medium of communication in the world today and its impact on people have been enormous.

This book Television and College Students is a research project prepared by Dr. Surojit Sen Gupta and is sponsored by the Indian Council of Social Science Research, North Eastern Regional Centre, Shillong.

In this study, Dr. Sen Gupta has carefully propped the theme on television viewing and its positive and negative impact on college students and he has identified six premier colleges in the city of Shillong for his study and interviewed in depth nearly three hundred students and has recommended some of the pointed findings in a lucid way.

I wish the findings of Dr. Sen Gupta reaches the attention of the communicators, policy makers, planners and administrators in order to evolve policies pertaining to the influence of personality development among the youth in Meghalaya and also in the Northeastern region of India.

C Joshua Thomas
Director
ICSSR-NERC, Shillong

Acknowledgements

The author expresses his thanks to the Indian Council of Social Science Research (North- Eastern Regional Centre), Shillong, for a generous grant to undertake this project. Without their financial help and encouragement, this study would not have been materialised.

My acknowledgement will remain incomplete if I do not thank Prof. A.C. Sinha (Former Professor of Sociology, NEHU), Shillong. It was his advice and encouragement that inspired me to take up this project as an independent researcher.

I am thankful to Ms. B. H. Buam, Lecturer (Selection Grade), College of Teacher Education (PGT) College, Shillong, for her valuable advice and suggestions. I will be failing in my duty if I do not thank all my well wishers more specially to my uncle Mr. Pranabendu Shekhar Sen Gupta, aunty Smt. Dolly Purkayastha, and Didi Ms. Susmita Ghosh, for their moral support and sustained encouragement.

My special thanks goes to Dr. (Mrs) Vardhini Bhattacharjee, Regional Director, IGNOU, Guwahati Regional Centre and Dr. K.S. Chakraborty, Regional Director IGNOU, Agartala Regional Centre for their valuable help and cooperation from time to time.

I also thank my Research Investigator Mr. Ricky for his help in completion of the project. Not to be overlooked are my respondents who positively responded to my questionnaire schedule – too many to be named. Without their cooperation, this work might not have been completed. I would also like to thank all those people whose names are not mentioned here, but directly or indirectly provided me help in carrying out this project work.

I must mention here the encouragement and support given by my brothers - Subhajit and Rajdeep and sister - Falguni. I am very much thankful to my friends and relatives, who always acted as a force behind the completion of this work. I do not have enough words to express my love and gratitude to my mother Smt. Bani Sen Gupta who have always been a source of inspiration to me.

I am thankful to Dr. C. Joshua Thomas, Director, ICSSR-NERC, Shillong for contributing his appreciation by writing Foreword to this work.

I would also like to extend my sincere thanks and gratitude to Mr. Pritam Das Gupta, who without hesitation, and within a very short period of time amidst his busy schedules was able to prepare the MSS to this book to the best of his ability. Last, but not the least, I can not refrain from expressing my appreciation of the help extended by Mr. M.P. Misra, Akansha Publishing House for cooperation to publish this book in elegant manner.

Dr. Surojit Sen Gupta

1

Introduction

Communication comes from Latin word 'Communico' which means sharing and not just sending messages. Therefore, communication is a social process, and countless ways in which human beings keep in touch with one another. The communication may be verbal, non-verbal, written, audio-visual etc. The act of communication suggests a sender (of message) a receiver. The message is what is communed between the two. The message is shared, reacted, non-reacted. When there is active communication, the effort is for interaction, interchange, dialogue and mutual understanding. Communication presupposes a shared symbolic environment, a social relationship among those who participate, leading to social interaction.

The messages in the shared environment could not only be oral, non-verbal, written, visual; but these could be laws, customs, practices, ways of dressing, gestures, buildings, gardens, exhibits, flags etc. Language and body synthesizers which are culture specific are essential components of messages. People in communication define the various types of society, sub-society and groups. Their characteristics depend upon the modes of communication they possess, media usage, rituals and signs of personal relationships.

The traditional concepts of communication is that we use communication to express our inner purposes, attitudes, feelings and to describe events and objects of the external world; to produce 'sharedness' between the speaker and the audience addressed. Another view is that patterns of social communication constitute the world as we know.

Communication is the locus of forces through which persons create and manage social realities. Social reality includes concept of self, community, institutions and cultures. Through communications we create conceptions of SELF - who we are; we create relationships within the community and build institutions. We communicate and act together to create, recreate community relationships. Relationships exist and are managed within a culture. Human communication notion is not always getting the accuracy of transmission but of social reality creation.

Defining Communication

Communication is defined in many different ways. Some explain it as an 'art' – something creative, while others say it is a science – a learned behaviour/skill. In a broader sense, communication is much more than an art. It is partly a skill and partly a science as it involves certain learnable techniques and psychomotor skills. However, communication is better described as a science because it is based on certain principles that can be verified and used to make it effective.

It is difficult to define communication through a single definition. Different people perceive it in different ways in the different contexts, provided by the various environments or surroundings where communication takes place. Starting from the sharing of meaning to persuading others to elicit the desired/intended responses, communication has been defined to suit situational purposes. At best communication is defined according to its components. There are three main components of communication: the source, the channel, and the receiver. From the source's point of view, communication is essentially persuasion, i.e., to assure communicator that communication has taken place, or the desired outcomes are achieved. From the receiver's point of view, communication is a process to elicit the desired responses. From the channel point of view, communication is a medium, a carrier of information from the source to the receiver and/or vice-versa. In other words, communication is defined in terms of the functions to be performed or the objectives to be achieved. According to Shanon and Weaver (1949) the primary concern of communication is to reproduce as faithfully as possible a message sent from one place to another place. Schramm (1973) defined communication as the functions of persuading, informing, teaching and entertaining people. Therefore, communication is a process by which create and share information with one another in order to reach a common understanding (Rogers, 1986).

Communication has been subjected to numerous and diverse conceptualizations. However, the key features of most definition are:

i) Human communication is a process of transmission of ideas, thoughts, feelings and behaviour from one person to another person.

ii) Communication is persuasive and seeks to obtain desirable response to what is being transmitted.

iii) Communication is a multiway process, two – way process.

There are several elements in the communication process. To generate communication there are five basic elements : sources, message, channel, receiver and effect of message. The communicator is the source of the message that he delivers to the people. The communicator can be the primary or secondary source of message. When he is secondary source of message he may get the information from other source who is more knowledgeable about the message. But it is the responsibility of the communicator to communicate it to the people in the form they can understand easily. To make communication effective, communicator must know the characteristics of the receiver/audience. A good knowledge of audience – their socio-cultural background, their needs, their problems, their limitations and level of comprehension will help the communicator to design an effective message. Source credibility is essential for effective communication. The communicator must have faith in what he is communicating; as well his audience must have faith in the communicator. Therefore, it is essential that the communicator must have adequate knowledge, information on the topic that he is communicating about.

Communication requires receivers and consumers of messages, the people with whom he communicates. A communicator must know his audience characteristics in general and specifically. The audience's characteristics, their background, past experience, learning abilities, interests, attitudes and values etc., can effects their receptiveness to the message conveyed as well as effectiveness of the messages. The effectiveness of any message will depend on the communication environment in which it is being conveyed or received. The communication environment may be conducive, hostile, appropriate or in appropriate. The main purpose of any communication programme is to produce an impact on a certain audience. The impact of any communication efforts can be assessed in relation to the objective of the communication act. There may not be any active communication unless there is dynamic inter-play of source, message, channel and audience to produce an effect.

Several factors contribute towards communication success at each level of communication. At the level of transmission factors such as media distribution, media capacity, media accessibility (both physical and social)media scheduling etc., and resources and accessibility of interpersonal communication channels contribute in ensuing transmission of communication messages. At the level of semantics, the CODE and STYLE used in message formulation are crucial. At the effectiveness stage, audience formulation processing behaviour, culture, tradition and other development inputs contribute in behavioural changes.

To ensure communication success, the communicator resorts to reinforcement of messages by repeated exposures, by detailed explanation of the messages. Motivation is another intervention used by the communicator to gain communication success. Motivation can range from simple persuasion to incentives through an educational process. Homophily between the source and the target audience can contribute to successful communication. Homophily is defined as the degree to which source- receiver pair is similar in certain attributes like beliefs, education, social status etc. Source credibility as held by the audience is another factor contributing towards communication success.

Functions and Process of Communication

Communication performs various socio-psychological functions. MacBride (1980) has discussed some functions of communication in a social system. The main functions of communication are:

(i) ***Information:*** Communication refers to collective storage and dissemination of information for wider utilization by people. In this way it enables people to participate in and take intelligent decisions on, any issues of social relevance. Information has been taken as a resource for development – socio – cultural and economic.

(ii) ***Socialization:*** Communication helps in‹.ividuals become active members of the society to which they belong. People learn social norms in order to live cohesively. Having access to a variety of information, individuals get opportunities to understand each other and appreciate other people's feeling, emotions, ideas and expectations in a social system.

(iii) ***Motivation:*** Motivation of the individual members of a society plays an important role for its development. Communication fosters the individual and community activities, and motivates the people to meet goals, which have been mutually agreed upon.

(iv) ***Education:*** Dissemination of information enhances the individual's intellectual development and helps one acquire the skills and aptitude required to become a productive member of society. In this way, communication and education are two sides of the same coin. The quality of education depends on the quality of communication between society and its members.

(v) ***Entertainment:*** Entertainment and recreation are important means of making individuals and society healthy. People find enjoyment and entertainment through various communication activities, viz., drama, dance, sports, music etc. These means of communication provides personal and collective enjoyment.

The process of communication most widely accepted is that of Shannon and Weaver (1949), which identifies five elements in the process, viz, the source, the receiver, the channel, a coding system and noise.

Source and Receiver: These two are the most important components of any communication process. No communication takes place without the source (i.e., the sender of information) and the receiver (i.e., the consumer of information). The source and the receiver could be human beings, animals or even non-living objects.

Channels: The means through which communication between the source and the receiver takes place are known as the medium or channel of communication. We communicate through various channels viz., by touch, by beating drums, through spoken words, through printed words, electronic gadgets etc. Even facial expressions can function as a verbal and non-verbal channels of communication.

The relationship among the source, the receiver and the channel can be diagrammatically represented thus:

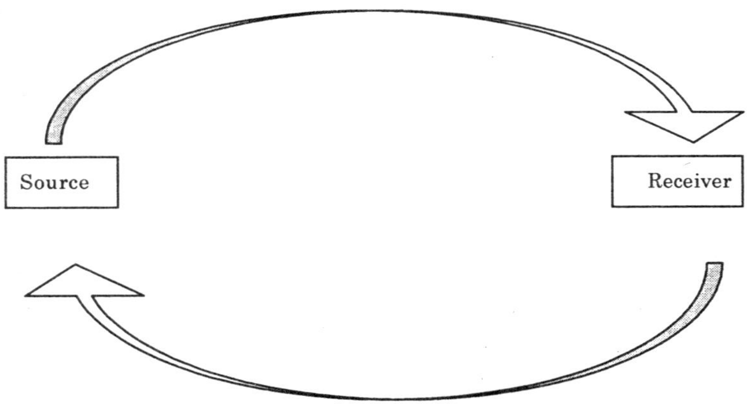

Channel

The channel is an important component of effective communication. There are two types of channels of communication-direct and indirect. In the direct channel of communication we use spoken words, facial expressions, physical postures and so on as channels for transmitting information and ideas. In the indirect channel, we use various electronic and non-electronic channels of communication.

Code: A communication code is a set of signals or symbols that creates meaning for both the source(s) and the receiver (Rogers, 1984). Word of mouth, written material, visuals, etc.,are codes that communicates ideas, views and feelings. There are several verbal and non-verbal codes that are use for communication. For successful communication the code used should be mutually accessible to the source and the receiver.

Noise: There are some factors that affects the smooth flow of communication. Those factors which disturb or interfere with the passage of information between the source and the receiver are termed 'noises' or 'barriers'. Thus, noise is the term that refers to any factor which prevents the proper exchange of information, apart from those caused by the sender and the receiver. It may be anything, such as technical problems in reception, over loaded information, etc.

Types of Communication

Communication occurs in many forms at different levels. These are categorized into three forms: Broad forms, Functional forms and Geographic forms. The three forms overlap and are convenient and practical categories.

Broad Forms of Communication: These forms of communication are Intrapersonal, Transpersonal, Interpersonal, Group communication, Mass Communication and Folk Communication.

Intrapersonal communication is communication with oneself. It is individual's reflection with oneself, contemplation and meditation. Transpersonal is communication with Divine through prayers, meditation etc. Interpersonal communication is face to face communication. It could be dydic, among a smaller or larger group of people. Thus group communication is essentially interpersonal. It could be formal like public meetings. lecture discussions and also non-formal like religious services, village markets, bazaars, melas, gossip groups, tea shop groups etc. Folk communication also called Traditional or popular media can be both interpersonal, group or mediated. The communication is through folk channels of songs, dance, theatre, religious discourses and mass religious meetings. Mass communication is mediated through such mass media channels as radio, television, cinema and press, video. This is essentially electronic media. Communication through mass media caters to the needs of the mass audience, for whom the messages are produced in mass, and distributed in mass, and are also consumed in mass. The distribution is done through these electronic mass media channels and even through traditional cultural media. The mass communication situation is mainly passive.

Functional Forms of Communication: Communication can be labeled as applied or theory related. Applied communication focuses on the practice of communication through various communication channels of mass media, interpersonal and folk channels. Applied communication has a social purpose, is action oriented and messages are communicated to create and implement practices. The different forms of applied communication include;

(a) Journalism through print and broadcasting media.

(b) Different types of messages through broadcast media of radio, T. V., video, cinema for informing, educating, and entertaining people.

(c) Development communication through mass media and interpersonal communication channels to focus on development practices and programmes.

(d) Communication through various communication technologies such as telephone, fax, satellites, computers etc.

Theory related communication focuses on conceptualization of communication theories and models of communication. Such deliberations form the basis of applied communication.

Geographic Forms of Communication: The geo related forms of communication between / among various ethnic groups; among various regions within a culture or ethnic groups. Intercultural communication is practised through mass media, interpersonal channels and folkways. Intercultural conceptualizations, theories and models are the foundation of intercultural communication.

There is multinational efforts towards globalisation of today's world through international communication for political, economic, social, development and defence reasons through mass media and interpersonal forums. Such communication deliberations develops international communication theories and models.

Communication Models

Communication models are visualisations of the communication process. They are basic theories concerning the elements of communication and how they operate and interact.

First, models organise the various elements and process of communication act in a meaningful and interesting way. Second, models aid in discovery of new facts about communication. It serves heuristic function. Third, models enable us to make predictions concerning communications, i.e., what will happen under certain conditions. Fourth, models may provide means of measuring the elements and processes involved in communication.

Linear Model of Communication: The earliest communication model was proposed by Aristotle - the Greek philosopher in his book *Rhetoric*. Aristotle's model presented is simple and linear. Aristotles included five essential elements of communication; the speaker, the speech or message, the audience, the occasion and the effects. In his book *Rhetoric*, Aristotle advises the speaker on constructing a speech for different audience on different occasions and for different effects. This model is actually more applicable to public speaking than interpersonal communication.

Lasswell Model of Communication: Lasswell proposed a communication model in 1948, which was not different from Aristotle's model presented 2300 years ago. Lasswell Model portrays the message flow in a pluralistic society in which there are numerous channels and multiple audiences. One could describe the pattern of message flow in modern society through this model.

Shannon and Weaver Model of Communication: Claude Shannon and Warner Weaver in Mathematical theory of communication model proposed a model in 1949. This model follows a left, to right process. The speaker selects a desired message from all the possible messages. The message is sent through a transmitter (a communication channel), and is changed into signals. The signals are received by the receiver. In the process of transmission certain distortions are added to the signal which are not part of the message send by the source and we call this NOISE.

This model led to technical improvements in this message transmission and it served to bring together scholars from several disciplines to study communication scientifically. The effort was towards a unified model of communication. But it failed since it did not consider the semantic or pragmatic levels of communication. Although Shannon and Weaver (1949) did discuss the semantic problem of the interpretation of meaning as compared with the intended meaning of the sender. Communication researchers who used this model did not give enough attention to 'Noise' and 'feedback' components.

Wendell Johnsons Model of Communication: Wendell Johnsons proposed one of the most insightful model in 1951. It is a simple model explaining the complex process of communication. According to Wendell Johnson there are five stages in communication process. The actual communication process begins at stage 1 which represents the communication event. This event is the external stimulus to communication. Although all communication may not have reference to this event. Johnson argues that communication makes sense when it relates to the external world. At stage 2 the receiver is stimulated through one or more sensory channels. At stage 3 the organismic evaluations occur. Certain bodily changes are effected like muscular tension etc. At stage 4, the feelings which are aroused at stage 3 are translated into words in accordance with individual's unique language habits. At stage 5 from all the possible linguistic symbols, certain ones are selected and arranged into a pattern.

At stage 1 the words that speaker utters or words that are written stimulate the receiver. Such an external event at stage 1 served as stimulation for the speaker.

At stage 2 the receiver is stimulated.

At stage 3 there are organismic evaluations.

At stage 4 feelings of the receiver are translated into words.

At stage 5 the linguistic symbols are selected and arranged.

At stage 1 these symbols serve as stimulation for another Receiver.

This is a continuous process. This model is not a complete explanation of communication process. It is rather an attempt to picture some of the most essential elements, processes and relevant relationships which make up the communication act.

But this model does serve as a frame work for 'interaction' component in the models that were developed later on.

Wilbur Schramms Models of Communication: The academic field of communication 'took off' when Shannon and Weaver (1949) set forth their model in their mathematical theory of communication. This model has much greater impact on the scientific study of communication than did Norbert Weiner's (1948) Cybernetic Model presented in the book CYBERNETICS. Evidently a linear model of communication fitted the needs of then emerging field of communication than the Cybernetic Model.

Wilbur Schramm was specially influential in facilitating use of linear models in 1950's and later on move to develop relational models in 1973. In his early research he used linear model in early form, i.e. Sender'→ Receiver model, later he realized the importance of 'Message' and so he used Sender'→ Message'→ Receiver model, still on further research the importance of channel was evidenced and he talked about Sender'→ Message'→ Channel'→ Receiver model. In 1970's his relational models were concerned with the effect on receivers. He used the 'effect' component and effect analysis from Berlo's model of 1960. Schramm implicitly suggested Interaction Component when he talked about active, selective and manipulative audience in his relational model.

Schramm (1971) argues that the most dramatic change in the general communication theory in the last 40 years has been the abandonment of the idea of a passive audience, and its replacement by the concept of a highly active and selective audience, manipulating rather than being manipulated by message – a full partner in the communication process.

Berlo's Model of Communication: David Berlo's model of communication (1960) explains the various components in the communication process. The four basic components are source, message, channel and receiver. For each of these four components there are five channels that need to be considered. The source and the receiver are treated in the same way. To study either we need to consider their communication skills (speaking and writing for the source, and listening and reading for the receiver), their attitude, their knowledge, the social system of which they are part, and the culture in which they operate. The message consists of both elements and structure, each of which may be broken down into content, treatment and code. For the channels, Berlo insists that the message may be sent or received through any or all of the five senses. It was for the first time that 'Effect' component was initiated in the communication process. Berlo suggested that message received must have some effect positive or negative on the audience.

Gerbner's Model of Communication: Gerbner's model of communication (1956) consideres these elements in the communication process: these is a source, an event, the source reacts to the event in a situation through some channel, the content and the consequences of the communication act are conveyed in some form and content. Gerbner's model emphasise the presentation of communication content through specific form and in specific context in which receiver receives the message.

Westley and MacLean Model of Communication: Westley and MacLean's model (1957) expanded on the Newcombs ABX model (A communicates to B on topic X) with the inclusion of 'C' as gatekeepers as developed by Lewin. The A's (communicators representing advocacy roles) select and transmit message purposely to modify the B's perception of X. The B's (perceivers and audience members representing behavioural system roles) respond in terms of their needs and requirement for message as a means of orienting themselves to the environment. The C's(representing channel roles or gatekeepers) are agents of the B's.Non purposively selecting and transmitting information for them. Feedback is an important component of this model.

DeFleur Model of Mass Communication System: The DeFleur Model (1966) expanded on the Shannon and Weaver model by interjecting a mass medium device and a feedback device; the latter to demonstrate that the communication process is circular. The 'noise' in the model may interfere at any stage in the mass communication process. DeFleur pictures the source, transmitter, receiver and destination as separate phases of mass communication process in much the same way as Schramm depicts in his early models.

Hiebert, Ungurait, and Bohn (HUB) Model of Mass Communication: In this model, the communication process is perceived as a set of concentric circles much like the waves formed when a pebble is thrown into a pool. The pebble, which is analogous to the communication content causes ripples that became ever widening circles until they hit the shore (audience) and bounce back (feedback). The idea is that initial content goes through a series of actions and reactions labelled as 'pool of human affairs'.

Vora's Model for Diffusing Concepts: The Vora's model is a complex model. It presents the concept of diffusion, knowledge, attitude change, and behaviour change in a dynamic and progressive spiral with utilizes mass media and interpersonal channels. This model emphasized the external and internal environment and effects components beside considering source, message, channel and receiver components in the mass communication process.

Non-Linear Models of Communication: The analytical concepts of interaction, self-generation, mutual exchange and sharing explain the human communication in Non-Linear models of communication.

The linear communication models of 1940's and 1950's were in fact foundation models and suggested new, useful and significant concepts which were later developed and integrated into Non-linear interaction, transaction and convergence models of 1980's.

The interactive communication models suggested that communication is not static but a process of action and reaction to what is said. By acting, reacting and interacting; we create patterns of communication functions. The functions could be phatic, creation of social realities, informing, educating and motivating people.

The linear communication models were useful for design of experiments which assumed one way casualty, for the study of propaganda and mass persuasion. This models describes a simple communication act and not the process of communication. Although Berlo in 1960's defined communication in terms of process but in his subsequent research, he did not pursue this idea. In fact Berlo (1977) acknowledge that S- M –C – R was not intended as a communication model but it was developed as an audio visual aid to stimulate recall of the components of communication relationships.

The Non-Linear models follow the cybernetic principle. The four most important elements of cybernetic explanation are the concept of information, feedback, networks and purpose.

Convergence Model of Communication: Kincaid (1979) developing the concept of feedback suggests that one – cycle feedback determines relative position of the sender and the receiver / s whereas two cycles feedback determines direction and rate of change of position.

Thus a three cycles feedback determines change in direction and velocity and four cycles feedback determines change in acceleration. Communication is thus a multistage information and decision process in which all participants may change their relative positions overtime, create and share information which can affect their relative position. Each stage in the process is contingent on the previous one.

An effective feedback process creates convergence and in effective feedback creates divergence. Convergence and divergence describe a change in position with respect to pre-determined goals. These goals can be understanding and mutual understanding which are fundamental to human communication. Human systems of communication comprise networks of individuals who share information, converge or diverge from one another in terms of mutual understanding of the reality.

Mass Communication

Mass communication is the outcome of amazing application of technology to extend the reach of the human voice. Mass media make it possible to deliver the same messages simultaneously to a vast and diversified audience, scattered far and wide. They are, simply defined, technical extension of the human voice much in the same way as the spade is an extension of the human arm. Mass communication requires an intermediate transmitter of information, a man medium – such as newspapers, books, magazines (collectively known as the print media), radio, television, film (collectively called the electronic media) or a combination of these.

A message can be communicated to a mass audience by many means. The printing press became available to the world in the fifteen century. But newer and faster means of mass communication came into being between 1896 when the films were invented and 1926 when the television first appeared. In course of only a thirty – year span, human ingenuity suddenly widened our ability to communicate by an incalculable degree. Technical marvels created by man conquered all the frontiers in a trice through the global diffusion of words, pictures and sounds. Nations of the world became more and more interdependent as the immediacy and the abundance of world wide communication provided a better understanding of the aspirations of other countries.

Mass communication is a process by which mass – produced messages are communicated through a mass medium to a large number of people. In primitive societies, the means of communication included such devices as drums, smoke signals etc. Similarly, the modern age has made available such media as printing, broadcasting, films to transmit information to a mass audience. Mass media, like the special gestures, are aspects of human communication. Mass media have far - reaching consequences for human society. Instant exchange of information and ideas among the people of the world has reduced human society to a global village. Every advance of technology has had the effect of broadening the reach of communication. Along with technology, the other prerequisites for the development of mass communication were, of course, mass literacy and development of transportation and communication system. Development in all these fields came about almost simultaneously to give an unlimited extension to the power to communicate.

Features of Mass Media Communication

Mass communication differs from interpersonal communication. The source of the message in mass communication is not a single person but a formal organization and the sender of the message is often a professional communicator. The message is not unique, variable and unpredictable but often manufactured, standardized, always multiplied in some way. The audience of mass media is not only a large one but one composed of people from varied social strata with very different norms of socio – economic behaviour and are scattered over a wide area. The individual receiver and the sender of the message in mass communication are not usually known to each other. The relationship between the sender and the receiver is uni-directional and necessarily impersonal. The impersonality results from the physical and social distance between the sender and the receiver.

Mass media convey information to countless people in different places. There is no certainty whether the message will be appropriate to their need or would be understood by the intended receivers. The sender in this case is an impersonal communicator who has very little personal knowledge about the socio-economic back ground of the receiver. The same message is being sent to all classes of people without any appreciation of its appropriateness.

The art of mass communication is obviously more difficult than face-to-face communication. Since the communication is addressing millions of people at the same time and with the same message, he cannot adjust or modify his message according to the actual need of the audience. An approach acceptable to a few, may not be appreciated by many. Mass communication provides information and tries to persuade but receives little feedback from its audience. The impact of the message is assessed through indirect or delayed feedback.

Mass media can be all - pervasive in its astonishing ability to conquer the physical barriers of the world, their actual accessibility and relevance in real terms are extremely limited. The majority of the people in the developing world remains at the periphery of the mass communication system due to object poverty and illiteracy. Mass media system is highly capital intensive and presupposes certain levels of education and economic resources. The greater number of people, therefore, have not yet received adequate mass media exposure to adopt it as part of their social and cultural environment.

Mass Media and its Functions

Mass media carry out a number of socially useful

functions. The most notable among these, of course, is keeping a close watch on every important development in the society and reporting events of public interest. This has been described as the surveillance function or close monitoring of the environment by media. The gathering and reporting of information is central to the surveillance of the environment.

Mass media have also been seen as a forum. It has an important function to correlate parts of the society in responding to the environment. Correlation refers to the interpretation of information through facts and opinions prescribing how people should react to these events. This function is carried out by the editorial writers, columnists, producers of documentaries and news analysis in television.

The mass media help to keep the culture and heritage of society alive and transmit it to others. They pass on social heritage by holding up a mirror to society, reflecting standards for behaviours, cultural values, social norms and folklore. Any communication becomes a part of the individual's accumulated experience or learning. It is this collective experience received through mass media that offers the pictures of cultural heritage of a country.

The entertainment function of the mass media is perhaps best appreciated. Entertainment refers to communicative acts primarily intended for amusement without necessarily offering any other functional values. It also reduces tension and make easier for people to cope with real life problems and for societies to avoid breakdown. But mass media often isolate people in their hours of entertainment and as a result, reduce socializing. Persuasion is another function of mass media in contemporary society. Persuasion is as significant as information and entertainment functions. Advertising, of course, is the most open form of persuasion but much of the persuasion in mass media is concealed and some even pass off as news.

While mass media perform certain socially useful roles, they may at times foster panic, create instability and promote anxiety or apathy. The socially positive correlation function of aiding mobilization, defining important issues and promoting efficiency through the assimilation of news may carry threats of increased social conformity, increased passivity and weakened critical faculties. Although mass media can take full credit for entertaining millions, they are also held accountable for lowering tastes, fostering passivity and permitting escapism.

Media are responsible for people's perception of reality, the "picture in our heads". But the picture one gets of the world is the product of the communicator's preference and perhaps, of prejudice. Mass media are primary source of information about issues but they do not always faithfully reflect all the reality. All mass media are controlled in some way by their sources. As media content passes, it is influenced by normal human bias and perception.

Mass media, as indeed all the means of communication, play a vital role in holding societies together specially in a country like India, passing through a process of change from traditional to modern systems of communication and cohesion. Nearly everywhere, the media are expected to advance national interests and promote certain key values but socially so, in times of crisis. Mass media play a significant role in national development. The process of planned development brings in its wake changes in values and attitudes and throws up a new set of problems on account of rapid industrialization. Mass media prepare the minds of the people to meet the challenge of these momentous changes. The functions of mass media in a developing country is to smoothen the peace of social transformation and to mobilize human resources behind national development.

Mass Media Theories

Theories of mass media developed from the studies of various mass media channels – Radio, T.V., Video, Camera,

Telephone, Telegraph, Fax, Gramophone, Audio cassette recorder, Press, Cinema, etc. Man has been able to expand fundamental interpersonal communication act into instantaneous public dissemination through mass produced and mass distributed messages. The messages are mass produced on these channels and the business of producing and transmitting vests with a few elites. These sources of messages are able to receive many receivers through many sense modalities instantaneously through instant feedback may be missing. In recent research the media is categorised under different heads to reflect the connection between media processes, and broader social and political relationships.

During the early years of the twentieth century, it was through by the scholars and researches in the area of mass communication that the messages of mass communication exert a powerful effect on the audience. This effect was thought to be direct and the messages of mass communication reach the audience directly, and exact a direct and compelling effect on the audience. This style of thinking has contributed to what is called as magic bullet theory of mass communication. This theory is also known as hypodermic model in mass communication. However, the research carried out by the scholars and researchers in mass communication have proved that the messages of mass communication has only limited effect on the audience. This has contributed to another theory or model that is known as limited effects model in mass communication. According to this model that the messages of mass communication media do not have direct one to one effect, but the media interacts with other segments of the society in influencing public opinion.

Paul Lazarsfeld, a well known political scientist and communication scholar has advanced a theory that is known as Two Step Flow Theory. According to this theory, the messages of mass media do not reach the audience directly. It first goes to opinion leaders, according to Paul Lazarsfeld.

Opinion leaders are those who occupy position of power and those whose opinion will considerably have some way over the masses. After reaching the opinion leaders such as doctors, scientists, engineers and politicians, it reaches ordinary people. Paul Lazarsfeld has done research in the radio and newspaper coverage of 1940 US presidential election in Erie, Chio and he has advanced this theory from his research.

Maxwell E. McCombs and Donald Shaw (1977) advanced the Agenda Setting Theory of mass communication. This theory holds that mass media suggest to people that which are the ideas are important and by themselves they are less effective in promoting particular attitudes than in determining which issues will receive peoples attention. This theory has come about as a result of research carried out by Maxwell E. McCombs and Donald Shaw. Most of the research in agenda setting has first involved abulating the amount of mass media exposure given to various topics. The audience were then surveyed as to how much importance they give to these topics. According to the researchers, these has to be correction between communication exposure and public relations to it. This comes out of the hypothesis held by the researchers. If there is any difference, then the researchers attributed it to individual differences.

Stanford University professor Everett M. Rogers (1982) has advocated a theory that is known as Social diffusion theory. According to this theory that new ideas spread in to a community goes through various phases before being accepted or not. According to him, this theory attempts to explain the relationship between the flow of new ideas in society and changes in attitudes and behaviour brought out by them. Rogers has done research in the area of spreading new information into an agrarian community and according to him people seen to go through a series of stages or steps in the process of adopting or rejecting new ideas. Rogers' theory of diffusion, although was well accepted in the academic circles in mass communication, is not without its critics.

The next important theory in the area of mass communication is the theory called dependency theory advocated by Melvin DeFleur and Sandra Ball-Rokeach (1982). This theory basically illustrates the difference between the way in which Sociologists and Psychologists analyse the communication process. According to this theory, that mass communications do not affect society as a one way process but that media, their audiences, and social structures mutually interact with each other. It is important that not only how media affects society but also how the society affects the media. The major application of dependency theory is that we do not use media separate from the influences of the society and the social system within which both the media and we co-exist. We are all or integral part of a social system and the social system has taught to us the way we should respond to media including what we have learned from the media itself. The basic premise of dependency theory is that we use mass media to learn more distant and complex parts of our society. The basic strength of this theory is that it is comprehensive. It provides an over all view rather than a narrow or myopic view of the relation of communication with public opinions.

Social Learning Theory propounded by Albert Bandura is an important theory in the area of mass communications. Albert Bandura is basically a psychologist and researched on the social psychological aspects pertaining to communication. Social learning is basically the observations of situations, individuals or behaviour that may affect our behaviour. In the context of mass communication theory, this means that learning acquired from media images and characterization. Albert Bandara has studied the prosocial and antisocial effects of television and has come to advance this theory in TV. He has studied the areas of TV and violence and children and has arrived at the social learning theory. Albert Bardura says that we learn both the positive and negative aspects through social learning. From the positive view point, social learning has contributed to the use of media for anti-cigarettes smoking campaign and other social welfare programmes. The other aspects of social learning is mainly from the TV and in this Albert Bandura discusses about the antisocial effects and the portrayal of various segments of society and violence in American Television. Although much of Albert Bardura is based on American context, his theory is still relevant to other countries as well as in the use of media in social learning.

George Gerbner and his associates Dr. George Gerbner, has advanced the media cultivation theory after considerable research in to the area of Television. According to him, TV cultivates reality by portraying images and people. We would have never visited a place in the world but we come to know of that particular place through television. Also, we watch TV everyday where violence is full of them, we would come to look at the world is being violent, infact it is not. This is the essence of Dr. Gerbner's research and he has pursued his research in two fronts. One is an annual analysis of the content of American primetime TV programmes. The other has been study of the differences in images held by heavy viewers and light viewers of American television. Dr. Gerbner hypothesised that those who watch TV heavily would say that the real world is full of violence. They called this TV answers because television exaggerates the number of people involved in violence. According to Gerbner, light viewers watch 4 hours of TV everyday and heavy viewers watch more than 4 hours of TV everyday. This is the type of research carried out by Dr. Gerbner to advance his media cultivation theory.

Psychologist, Leonard Berkowitz advanced the Aggressive Stimulation Theory. According to this theory, an individual tends to behave in aggression found to increase if; (1) violence is in depicted in the medium, (2) it seems just liable, (3) and the individual saw a similarity between the depicted violence and a situation that he or she had faced or experienced. Fredrick Williams (1984) says in his *New Communication* that Berkowitz Aggressive Stimulation Theory places much more emphasis on likely interactions between the context of the depicted aggression and circumstances and attitudes of the individual. This means that a person is likely to behave in aggression, if he is likely to watch aggression in TV and sees similarity between the situation portrayed in television and reality.

Elihu Katz (1960) at sociologist in Israel advanced the uses and gratification theory, that attempts to describe and explain how people use different communications media to satisfy their personal and social needs. Katz has assembled five basic needs such as cognitive, psychological integrative, needs strengthening contact with the family and lastly tension releasing or escapment needs. He questioned 1500 Israelis on these needs and the degree to which they use mass media for fulfilling their needs. He has come to the following conclusions.

(i) That the non-media situations of communication were related as more valuable than the individual media uses.

(ii) Mass media was considered useful for topics that are away from their immediate environment.

(iii) Media was considered useful for;

   (a) escapist needs,

   (b) needs required comparative information,

   (c) self oriental needs.

(iv) TV was more popular than books for gratification among less educated.

The uses and gratification research was an important area of study among the theories of mass communication.

Marshall McLuhan (1964) a Canadian professor in the area of mass communication has written three books, *The Gutenberg – Galaxy*, *The Mechanical Bride* and *Understanding Media*. In his books and writings he has emphasised on the power of the media. According to him, the media are more powerful than the message that they communicate to the people.

Each one of the above theory of mass communication attempts to answer a particular set of questions relating to media and its effects or application on society.

Effects of Mass Media

The objectives of mass mediated messages is intellectual and cultural enrichment. The requirements of different population, groups and strata influence the culture of everyday life. These are significant for managing social processes. The media effects can be answered in terms of creating awareness, knowledge, attitude and behaviour change; impact on value systems and ideology of society and creating tripartite relationship between media audience and society.

Sondhi Krishen (1985) is of the opinion on that awareness level in all segments of society has gone up because mass media of today is assuming powerful role. But the pervasiveness of mass media is having undesirable effects on our value system. Value system is identified with sensitivity to human conditions. He argues in favour of Holistic model of mass communication ideology to counteract the eroding of value system through various new communication models. Such a model rejects the technological model as it focuses on only monologue whereas dialogue communication is necessary. The holistic model emphasises commune with the audience, connection and inter – subjectivity. The second major problematic aspect of current situation in mass media is the nature of masscom contents. In India mass-com contents there is overtopicality with politics, lack of investigative perspective, planned propaganda bias given to development communication and total bureaucratisation of development communication.

Narula (1993) observed that in India, the endeavour is to make mass media contents more entertainment-oriented. Research evidence is that specifically on India T.V. the entertainment oriented programmes do not reflect the enriched cultural taste of India. Not only such mass media contents expose public to a lower cultural level now but in years to come it will mould their level to that cultural taste only. Narula (1993) emphasised that mass media channels are mirrors and moulders of ideology. Therefore, the ideology of society as well as ideology of the communication channels is mutually dependent on each other. We may use mass media channels as ideological apparatuses for inculcating social idealism but the projection of the social realities of the masses can not be ignored.

DeFleur and Rokeach (1982) discusses the Dependency theory of media effects. The proposition is that: the potential for mass media message to achieve a broad range of cognitive, effective and behavioural effects will increase when media systems provide many unique and central information delivery services. The potential will be further increased when there is structural instability due to conflict and change in society. The altering audience's cognitive, affective and behavioural conditions can feedback to alter both society and media. Thus there is tripartite relationship between media, audience and society.

DeFleur and Rokeach further suggests that the media effects is in terms of change in beliefs systems and attitudes and values. The attitudes formation towards a constant flow of new topic, a subtle shift in the value system. Another cognitive effect may be media role in agenda setting. Agenda setting is an interactional process. The topics are selected by the media, presented to the public. Information about such topics is selectively assembled and selectively disseminated. The public sorts out the issues and information selectively. Another cognitive effect that occurs is the expansion of people's system of beliefs. The people's knowledge and belief system expand because they learn about other people, places and things from mass media. There is impact of media on values. Media information cannot change the basic values but they play significant part in creating conditions for clarifying the values. One way that media creates value clarification is by presenting information that precipitate value conflicts with audience members. Once the mass mediated information identify and clarify the value conflict; the audience members articulate their own value positions. In this process even genuine value priorities became clarified.

Klapp Orrin (1972) has proposed that the nature of media information has substantial effects on people's morale and alienation in societies where media play central communication roles. People who rely on mass media systems as primary source of information about their groups and categories can thus experience changes in level of morale and alienation when there are notable changes in the quantity or quality of the information delivered by the media.

Larsen Otto N. (1964) discusses the Activation and Deactivation effects of the overt behaviour of media. The Activation Effect refers where audience do something as a consequence of receiving media messages. They may engage in issue formation or issue resolution as a consequence of attitudes that they have formed and the feelings developed because of media messages. The media messages may activate people to be pro-social or antisocial according to the media messages they receive. Deactivation effects refers to what people would have otherwise done but they do not do as a consequence of media messages.

The integrated model of media effects presents a complex set of variables and factors that generate as well as inhibit media influences. Yet within this complex system, mass communication effects are generated.

Gozzi (1985) addresses the mass media effect in High context and Low context cultures. Hall (1973) identified Low context cultures as developing countries and High context cultures as developed world. Gozzi further discusses the fact that the mass media has been invented and involved within Low context cultures. The hypothesis is that in a Low context cultures, media provides context. It is suggested that media function differently in High context culture. In High context culture media provides a 'distant context' describing the world outside the boundaries of the High Context culture but being interpreted by the categories of the culture.

Effects of mass media in Low and High context cultures: Low context cultures provide culture context through mass media. The cultivation research of Gerbner and his colleagues (Gerbner et al. 1980) demonstrates the fact that people do use mass media representations to fill in their pictures of social reality. Another line of research that illustrates the process of providing context is Agenda Setting (McCombs and Shaw 1972). Third line of research is supported through the word of Elizabeth Noelle-Neumann (1974). Her studies document the influence of media in creating "spiral of silence". By emphasising certain opinions media can create the impression that most of the people have that opinion on that issue. This in turn creates a tendency for people who oppose that opinion to remain silent even if they are a majority.

Beltran (1976) pointed out that the tendency of the Low context researchers is to focus on individuals as unit of analysis rather than larger social units. As Rudolph and Rudolph (1966) pointed out that in Low context cultures the unit of opinion is more likely to the extended family, the sub-caste, the village etc., than the individual opinion on many subjects, and is often the product of group traditions or deliberations.

The High context culture use its interpersonal networks to interpret media images. In a Low context culture the interpersonal networks is smaller or even absent and mostly the burden of interpretation fall on the individual. The High context culture have a stock of cultural symbols and stories to deal with the alternative symbols and stories coming from the mass media.

Media creates a pseudo-environment (context) and this pseudo-environment will be seen far and away and outside the High context culture. In Low context culture, in contrast, the pseudo-environment may be taken for real. In High context culture or sub-culture the media messages will be accepted, some will be rejected, and most will undergo some form of distortion. Even with the distortion of cultural interpretation media provides an "extension of the boundaries of the world" to High context cultures.

The High context culture exposed to mass media will have to deal with new symbols and new information; and these will change the culture somewhat through opinion varies about the degree of change. It seems plausible that mass media will produce greatest effect in relatively Low context cultures within the High context cultures such as in growing cities, groups of immigrants, or sub-cultures deviant from the mainstream and they need to know new social ways of being. For them, the contexting, effects of mass media will be powerful. For the people in the relatively High context parts of the Low context culture the contexting effects of the media are removed to the outside and that media imagery would effect them less.

Thus, mass media functions differently in Low context cultures and High context cultures and that the media functions and effects in both types of the world need to be studied by different means. The media has the potential for either reinforcing or undermining cultures or doing both at the same time.

Television as a Means of Mass Media

It is widely believed that mass media has an important role to play in achieving national goals. The UNESCO report on various aspects of communication and society provides eight following functions of mass media;

(1) Dissemination of information;

(2) Socialization;

(3) Motivation;

(4) Promoting debates and discussion on public issues;

(5) Education;

(6) Cultural promotion;

(7) Entertainment; and

(8) Integration.

And television, the newest electronic medium, performs all these functions effectively and with perfection.

Television is one of the nicest inventions of man. It has an edge over other forms of mass media, viz, radio and newspapers etc. It has overcome the barrier put up by illiteracy, which is the main hurdle with the print media. It provides a unique communication process, in a way helping mass communications becoming very simple and speedy. It is a multi-media system predominated by the visual medium. It is recognised that there is an urgent need for mass education and communication media for accelerating social change, creating awareness and inculcating scientific temper among the masses. It will also inculcated desired attributes and attitudes among the masses necessary for national development.

Television, the powerful medium of communication, is a produce of the ongoing modern communication revolution. It commands bigger influence on the perceptions, emotions and the outlook of the masses than any other media. The impact of television on the society is often compared with the effect of " water dripping on a stone, steadily, imperceptibly eroding old values and attitudes in favour of new ones" (Joshi, P.C., 1983). McLuhan (1967) holds that television is the most appropriate medium for mass communication specially for the developing countries because of its involving and absorbing nature.

Strategy and Method of the Study

Need and importance of the study

Over the last few decades, attempts have been made by communicators, policy makers, planners and administrators to study the concept, correlation and issues of media and development. The dramatic leap in communication technology has bestowed wider dimensions to today's social and political communication.

One such media is Television. Television has significantly altered our lifestyle in several ways in the span of a few decades. For many years, Doordarshan, the government owned channel was the only medium of entertainment. Now there are many channels which supposedly provide variety and choice to viewers. In reality, however, what TV channels show is influenced partly by what the government dictates and largely by what the sponsors feel is right. TV has penetrated so deeply into the modern life, that it is setting the agenda and influencing the viewers. The proliferation of the electronic media is not only having a pervasive impact influence in our private lives but also to an extent a perverse influence in more senses than one.

Considering the cultural differences across continents, a few channels from the affluent countries have begun to have such a profound influence on us that it could be said that the medium has become the message. Media is seen to create gender and generational conflict across cultures.

The telecommunication revolution has shrunk distance and space and made it possible to access views and news anywhere almost instantaneously. This has, in many ways, been a boon in shaking and strengthening the democratic institutions. In life, the bad comes with the good. The question is how can we optimize the positive elements of the Television and minimise the negative effects, particularly the disparate one. There is no dispute about the positive role of the Television. Similarly there also exists not merely a consensus but a growing concern about its harmful effects. However, positive effects do not stick so easily and negative affects do not leave us so readily. Therefore, it is useful and appropriate to focus on the impact of Television Viewing among the college students of Shillong at their highly impressionable age.

Objectives of the study

Television viewing as it is apparent now a days, has become a prominent part of daily life. It has emerged as the most potent and popular communication medium. The double appeal of Television because of both, audio and the visual media has literally succeeded in keeping people glued to it. Due to its visual effects, sound effects, music, pictures and animations, television is being used as entertainment, informative and educative media. That is why it is said that television has become an integral part of every person's life. Especially youngsters are connected with it very much. The high rate of television ownership and a twenty-four hours variety broadcast on account of satellite transmission lead to the constant exposure of youngsters, both from within and outside their society. Charm of television viewing is so much that youngsters use to adjust their times for studies and other activities to compensate for the time spent on television viewing. There may be variation in the duration of televiewing, types of the television programme viewed by them, intensity of parental control and companionship at the time of televiewing. On the context of the above background the present study is felt imperative to gage the impact of televiewing on college students in the most cosmopolitant city of North East, i.e., Shillong. Thus it is proposed to study the following aspects of television viewing on college students of Shillong:

1. To understand the positive impact of Television among the college students.
2. To find out the negative aspects of watching Television.
3. To examine the influence of Television on personality development.

Delimitations of the Study

The study was conducted only on six colleges, viz., (a) St. Edmund's college, (b) St. Mary's college, (c) St. Anthony's college, (d) Shillong college, (e) Sankardev college, and (f) Women's college, in Shillong. The study could cover a wider area, but owing to paucity of time and for the sake of convenience, the study was conducted only to a limited area. Nevertheless, despite the limitations it is optimistic of the fact that the findings of the study would yield, would provide a platform from where inferences could be made and conclusions would be drawn on the larger content.

Construction and finalization of the questionnaire

The questionnaire was constructed carefully in the light

of other questionnaires which were available. The questionnaires thus constructed were both closed and open ended. The close type was selected because of the fact they were easy to respond, they take little time, they keep the respondent on the subject and they are fairly easy to tabulate and analyse.

The questionnaire was first tried out on 25 respondents from the college students under study in the month of August 2006, in order to determine the suitability of the instrument. After getting back the try out questionnaires, the investigator thus felt the necessity of improving and validating the questionnaire. Accordingly the questionnaire was revised and some needed modifications were incorporated.

After analyzing the items on the basis of expert criticism and in the light of try out results, the next step was to administered the questionnaire and to collect the desired data for carrying out the present study. The final administration of the questionnaire was done in the month of September to November 2006.

Sampling design and field strategy

We have made use of the sampling technique for collection of primary data. The universe of this study comprised of six degree colleges out of many colleges in Shillong, viz., St. Edmund's College, St. Anthony's College, St. Mary's College (Christian Missionarie institutions and also known as elite institution) and Women's College, Shillong college, Sankardev College (Non-Christian Missionaries-non elite institutions). All these colleges are situated in Shillong city and come under the jurisdiction of the North- Eastern Hill University (NEHU) Shillong.

The respondents for the study were the Degree students of First Year, Second Year and Third Year from three streams, i.e., Arts, Science and Commerce. By using random sampling method, 300 students were selected, that is 50 students from each college. These were taken, as the investigator considered the students of these colleges to represent that class in society who are the most vunerable to the audio-visual media.

The chosen techniques for identifying the respondents led to 300 from all the six colleges. The respondents were served with the questionnaires and their responses on them were collected in course of time. After collecting back the questionnaire, we found that some answers in the questionnaire were vague and incomplete. With a view to removing distortions from our analysis, we decided to exclude such incompletely answered questionnaires. And that how we managed to get a list of 277 completed questionnaires for statistical analysis.

For secondary sources, the collection of information was based on the review of relevant literature, journals and magazines, newspapers, research works, books etc. Thus, both primary and secondary sources of data were used to understand the impact of television viewing on college students in the city of Shillong.

2

Development of Television

Television has been called everything from an educational panacea to 'the chewing gum of the eye'. People have lebelled it biased, accurate, liberal, conservative, and have accused it of everything from wrecking a family structure to robbing us of our individuality. Somewhere in between all this lies the truth. But one thing is certain. Today the medium had become one of the most powerful communicative forces in the history of technological civilization. Today satellites cross paths in space to transmit TV pictures from one country and culture to another. It has come of age as a world medium.

Television - Early Development

To fully appreciate the great technological strides television has made in the past decades, we need to examine the history of the medium.

The concept of television has been traced back to 1839. In that year the French physicist Alexander Edmond Becquerel observed the electrochemical effects of light. In 1884,the German Scientist, Paul G, Nipkow, devised a method whereby a spiralling disc could pass over a picture and create a scanning effect. Nipkow transferred the light passing through each light into electrical energy and transmitted this electrical energy through wires to a receiver which had a synchronized disc connected to a transmitter. When the transmitter changed pictures at rapid intervals, a very crude picture with semblance of motion could be achieved.

A breakthrough came in 1923 with Russian physicist Vladimir Zwonykin's patent of the iconscope tube television camera. In Zwonykin's invention, electricity picked up where mechanics had left off. His process used electrons to scan lines in a sweeping motion. The electron scanning process increased the optical clarity of a picture as compared to the mechanical process. Changing of pictures and the using a fast scanning process results in a clear vision of motion. This illusion is created because motion is not inherent; it is only one's eyes and brain that lends the illusion of motion.

When one looks at an object, in an interpersonal communication, the eye becomes the receiver of visual stimuli which are transmitted via the optic nerve to the brain. When one looks at an object, the brain retains the impression of that object for a fraction of a second. Since television projects images more rapidly than what the eye and brain can comprehend the television pictures being scanned for a fraction of a second creates an illusion of motion. And because television pictures change so rapidly that one cannot possibly perceive the movement, the illusion is of smooth motion.

In 1925, an Amercian named Jenkins Gnese demonstrated a mechanical television apparatus. An experimental television programme was sent by wire between New York and Washington by Bell Telephone Laboratories in 1927. Next year the same laboratories experimentally televised outdoor programmes. Simultaneous speech, music and picture transmission became a reality.

In 1936, the first regular television service in the world was started by the British Broadcasting Corporation (BBC). The public of the United States had its first view of television in operation at the World Fair in New York city in 1939. Thirty years later an estimated 500 million persons watched on TV as earthmen first set foot on the moon in 1969. In 1972, a large television audience viewed the summer Olympic Games. Electronic signals, mostly video-taped and timed to reach maximum audience, were transmitted by a satellite to approximately 100 countries.

A similar process takes place in colour television, as it does in the black and white television. Again one's intra-personal communication enables one to see colour. The eye actually has the capacity to intercept three primary colours-red, blue, and green. Combinations of these wave lengths of light are responsible for all other colours. In colour TV, a separate tube detects each of these primary colours in an image and each transmits its results to a TV receiver. The eye and brain then sees a cohesive picture based on tiny elements of red, blue and green appearing on the television screen.

Development of Television in India

Experiments with television began in India as early as 1959. To start with, the scope of programmes was restricted to educational broadcasts for a limited area around New Delhi. The programmes were primarily meant for medium and high school students, and were beamed at publicly funded schools in and around New Delhi which were provided with television receivers in classrooms. The principal goal of these programmes was to supplement classroom based education. In addition, there were some programmes meant for farmers in the agricultural areas around the capital. There were also some 'entertainment' programmes to supplement these broadcasts which were primarily based on Hindi feature films. At that time the variety of programmes was limited.

The production and transmission facility was based in New Delhi. It was a part of the existing radio transmission centre to All India Radio. At that time the 500 – watt transmitter operates in the evenings for one hour on Tuesday and Friday. Since transmission technology was still new in India, and because most of the receiving sets were located in Community Centres, television viewing remained primarily a community affairs with specific instructional aims. Television, at this initial phase, was not considered to be medium of entertainment but primarily a pedagogic tool. Given this principal purpose of television, the institution was also financially supported by the government.

The government provided the necessary funds to maintain these experimental broadcasts. Not only did the government, through the Ministry of Information and Broadcasting, determine what was to be put on the air, but they also sponsored the production of programmes and the running of studios. Most of the community television receivers were also provided by the government, and television remained very much under state control. The forty minute transmissions were sponsored by the government, and the studio was operated by a handful of engineers who were also programme developers, directors and camera operators. By the mid of 1965, broadcasts had been expanded to a daily one hour programme. The material of broadcast was still primarily instructional fare. However, the variety of the instructional medium had increased. There were now more programme for school children. Similarly, agricultural programmes were longer and covered a larger range of concern. Television was beginning to be considered a useful tool for information for the large community of farmers, particularly in the regions around New Delhi.

In the latter part of the Sixties, there were rapid developments in the television infrastructure in India with the building of a spacious auditorium as a annexe to the Broadcasting House of All India Radio (Akashvani Bhawan) in New Delhi. By 1972, the Delhi Centre was telecasting every evening between 6:30 and 10:30. The programmes were a mix of educational material and items based on feature films. Moreover, television receiver technology was being indigenously developed and an increasing number of domestically built Black and White sets were available in the market. This led to the acquisition of personal sets, and the earlier practice of community viewing was increasingly replaced by the growing popularity of the television set among upper and upper-middle class households in Delhi.

The period between 1972 and 1982 saw the rapid expansion of television in India. Two aspects of television that saw dramatic changes in this decade were the proliferation of programmes on television and rapid developments in production and transmission technologies. The educational fare of the sixties was increasingly supplemented by a large variety of other programmes. These included sports, news, feature film based music programmes, television plays made for Doordarshan, foreign comedies and a large number of programmes that were produced for television by people who worked primarily in the medium of television. Earlier, programmes were produced by people trained in the media of cinema and radio, but now, more and more people trained in television were involved in production. All this did not, however, replace the existing educational programmes for school children and farmers, but supplemented them, and often reproduced them in more attractive ways. There was, thus, a shift in the nature of television, as its didactic image was supplemented by the image of a medium which would bring home the live broadcast of a cricket test match or offer the luxury of watching Hindi and regional films in one's living room.

The significance of these developments was in the richness of the emerging programmes structure on television. What was initially an educational medium with a set of standardized programmes, with head and shoulder lectures on a variety of subjects, was replaced with the more imaginative use of talent to present similar material in more attractive formats. This included the emergence of programmes such as talk shows, quizzes and dramatization, that would address issues of education and family planning but would do so in a way that was more specific to the narrative, representational style of television.

At the same time, there were great advancements in the production and distribution technologies of television. There was an increase in the number of broadcast facilities as local television stations were set up in most metropolitan areas. There was also a proliferation of repeater stations, bringing even small towns under the umbrella of local broadcast facilities. Indeed, television was producing a new geography of India, with yet another axis of differences: those who has access to television and those who did not. Although, within the next decade, most of India was brought under the umbrella of television, there was a point when there were large parts of India that could not have access to the medium. Interestingly, the Indian Government was quick to realize that in certain parts of India there was competition between Indian and foreign broadcasts. It was, thus no accident that the two metropolitan areas that were first to have local broadcast facilities were Jalandhar in Punjab and Calcutta in West Bengal.

Thus, television had become a common household artifact. Most middles class urban homes were able to afford one television set per household, and television began to play a central role in redefining domestic space and time.

Given the centrality of the medium in the Indian household, it was often the focus of attention in the evenings when daily transmissions would take place. Family viewing of television as a leisure activity became increasingly popular.

The significant aspects of these changes were in the proliferation and availability of telecasts across most of the country; the diversity of programmes on television leading to the possibility of indentifying similar and conflicting sets of programmes. These trends, along with the increasing presence of entertainment programmes and the developments in both broadcast and receiving technology, brought dramatic changes to the state of television in the period following 1982.

Following 1982 and the ASIAD games, television in India developed as a medium whose earlier 'educational' purpose and programming was increasingly supplement by the growing presence of non-educational programmes. This progarammes diversified from the earlier dependence on feature-film based programmes into television plays and the emergence of serials. By 1984-1985, there was a rich variety of programmes in India. Some of the earlier programmes, such as informative talk shows, quiz programme, educational and entertainment programmes, film-based programmes and sports programmes were retained. But, supplementing these, there emerged a large range of programmes that included serialized narratives, news reviews, teleplays, and a greater variety of educational programmes.

This diversity was the emergence of a television flow, as the evening broadcast comprised a stringing together of a large number of programmes of different kinds, interspersed with commercials. This differed greatly from the earlier arbitrary juxta-position of educational broadcasts. The variety of programmes now followed each other in specific patterns beginning with the early evening children's programmes, moving on to programming for women and youth, followed by news and then a string of serialized programmes that occupied the so-called 'prime time' of Indian television broadcast which was initially from eight in the evening till ten at night. Given the fact that India has only one time zone, there was no question of staggering programmes or having different sets of programmes in different regions. The National Network went on the air around eight in the evening with the Hindi news indicating the beginning of prime time. Through these programmes expansions, the development of a recognizable flow, and the emergence of specific progarammes such as the Ramayan and Mahabharat, Doordarshan developed its own set of cultural and signifying practices that were specific to television in India. This was made up of programme variety and the scheduling.

In most parts of India, the broadcast was broadly divided between the material coming from the local transmitting station and the National Network programmes originating in Delhi. This established a conflicting relationship between the regional broadcasts and the centralized national broadcasts. A majority of the serials were a part of the National Network. Further, the broadcasts from Delhi were primarily in Hindi. The regional stations carries the local language broadcasts. Also, there was only one channel of broadcast where the time was shared between the regional and National transmissions.

The duration of broadcasts were constantly increasing. By early 1989, there were three large segments of broadcasts on weekdays and Saturdays. Typically, there was an hour long broadcast in the morning starting at seven. The programmes included a news sections, which contained a brief weather report and forecast. In addition, there were a series of public service announcements, short skits, a couple of songs and a closing brief news segment. This was a part of National Network. The second series of broadcasts were in the afternoon, starting around one and continuing till about four. These were primarily educational broadcasts of the National Network. Finally, there was the evening broadcast which lasted till about eleven at night. This period was divided into two segments – the regional broadcasts and the National Network which began around eight with the Hindi news followed by the evening's fare. Commercials were interspersed across the evening. However, commercials were always placed between programmes and did not interrupt any programmes.

It is also during this period that there was a proliferation of both transmission and receiving technology in India. The key developments followed the ASIAD games which were broadcast in colour, using a variety of microwave and satellite links to reach a large part of the nation. This was the beginning of the expansion of televison's coverage, and most of the country was soon brought under the umbrella of the National Network that carried the bulk of television progrmmes in India. Increasingly, the programmes were produced and broadcast in colour, and there was a boom in the manufacture of colour television sets, and more and more households began to switch to colour receivers.

Software Policy for Television

The development of television system in India was emphasised by the eminent scientist, Vikram Sarabhai. Not only did he understand the importance and potentiality of television in India context, he provided a perspective for television. In Sarabhai's opinion the major issues in developing a TV system in India are:

(1) Whether facilities of TV should first go to the city or to the village? He emphasized the need "to take effective steps to enrich life in the isolated rural communities". He realised the urgent necessity of television in performing the role of "a common mass medium of communication" which can reach all the people irrespective of age, sex, illiteracy, literacy and privileges. This can help in achieving national integration and stability of India. In his view, telecasting by setellite would be an advanced technology and would be economical and suitable to Indian conditions.

(2) "In a state of economic and social backwardness, do we need to deploy imaginatively the most powerful techniques at our disposal or can we get by with less

effective means? He pointed out that TV can make a unique contribution for it is gifted with unmatchable credibility and rare persuasive quality.

(3) "Can we regard TV largely as an instrument rather than overhead of society? The answer to this question depends clearly on how we use the medium and who uses it?" Sarabhai suggested that the "objectives and assumptions" of the decision-makers are the determining factors. He was against the idea of control of policies as well as programming content to be exercised by one set of people.

(4) He was aware of the responsibility of various governmental agencies like "information and broadcasting, education, agriculture, health, family planning, etc." But he was worried about how these different agencies could manage the TV system effectively along with promoting their own assigned goals. The solution he thought was that each agency should buy time from TV according to their needs.

(5) He cautioned "since the Government has a very powerful rôle in promoing development, how can one prevent bureaucratisation of the system of mass communication with television? What would be the organisational framework in which programming initiative can be developed competitively amongst independent groups of innovative and imaginative producers and artistes instead of through a monopolistic system where just a few official units produce all the programmes that are required?" He suggested that India should have a TV system based on ten lines of INTELSAT in the international arena, which only "owns regulates and manages", and it should not take the whole burden of software. In order to cater to the needs of software for developmental communications

an "evaluation system" and a "feed-back system" should be created.

The other important point concerning television was the question of accessibility. Sarabhai made a strong plea for provision of community TV sets both for rural and urban clusters of population. The urgent need for providing community TV sets was emphasised by both the Verghese Committee and the Joshi Committee.

Policy Guidelines

The Television medium is based on psychological principles. According to the mass communication theories, people take the assistance of mass-media to confirm their ideas, beliefs and convictions. The psychological effects may be positive or negative depending on the individuality of the viewer. Hence the Ministry of Information and Broadcasting has formulated certain policy for the proper functioning of TV.

Coverage to government's programmes, publicity to developmental programmes, important to rural population programmes to eradicate social evil, balanced coverage of news and other features and coordination between different media units are some of the important guidelines. While giving free hand in its programming the policy guidelines imposed certain restrictions and also make it clear that the broadcast media has to operate very cautiously. The AIR Code, which also applies to Doordarshan, was adopted in 1968 and revised in 1970 states that Broadcasts will not permit:

1. Criticism of friendly countries;
2. Attack on religion or communities;
3. Anything obscene; or defamatory;
4. Incitement to violence or anything against maintenance of law and order;

5. Anything amounting to contempt of court;
6. Aspersions against the integrity of the president, Governors and Judiciary;
7. Attack on political party by name;
8. Hostile criticism of any state or the centre; or
9. Anything showing disrespect to the Constitution or advocating change in the Constitution by violence; but advocating changes in a constitutional way should not be debarred.

The SITE

The Satellite Instructional Television Experiment (SITE) is an important landmark in growth of TV in India. During the SITE, the possibilities of TV as a catalyst of change for the rural population in remote locations were explored with specially designed programmes on education and social awareness. It remains hitherto the largest experiment in human communication for national development. It was also a big leap forward in the application of satellite technology for development and education. The broad objectives of the SITE were spelt out by Dr Vikram Sarabhai in these words : "If India wants to reduce the overwhelming attraction of immigration to cities, enrich rural life,integrate the country by exposing one part to the cultures of the other parts, involve people in the programme of rural, economic and social development, then the best thing is to have TV via a satellite".

The SITE was conducted in 2,400 villages, spread over 20 districts in the six economically backward states from August 1975 to July 31, 1976. It used a satellite to beam instructional programmes on agriculture, health and primary education simultaneously in the four major languages in Bihar, Orissa, Madhya Pradesh, Andhra Pradesh , Rajasthan and Karnataka. Besides, about 400 villages in Gujarat also received these programmes through a transmitter set up the Indian Space Research Organisation (ISRO) at Pij.

To conduct the experiment, the National Aeronautical and Space Administration (NASA) of the United States made available to India Applications Technology Satellite-6 (ATS-6), a very powerful and sophisticated satellite for just one year. The NASA had the responsibility for the space craft and the ISRO looked after the ground segment. The ISRO built two ground (earth) stations at Ahmedabad and Delhi to transmit and receive signals to and from the satellite. The software was entirely handled by the All India Radio (AIR) with three TV studios for production of special programmes in four languages at Cuttack, Delhi and Hyderabad.

The SITE was preceded by study of national development needs, the possible approaches and its technical and economic aspects. The programmes were planned in collaboration with the agriculture, health, education and social welfare authorities. The objectives of agricultural programmes were to provide information about improved farming methods, market trends and weather forecasts. The programmes also covered health and child welfare. The school broadcasts were designed for primary and pre-primary students in order to create interest in learning by providing colour and excitement in the dull and drab atmosphere of the village schools.It was intended as an enrichment programme and not tied to any syllabus. Entertainment in the form of drama, dance and music. Particularly folk art forms completed the fare.

Viewing on a mass scale in the SITE, villages was made possible through the specially provided community sets. On an average 172 villagers watched the programme per set per day which worked out to about 3.36 lakh viewers per day, assuming that only 84 per cent sets were working on any given day. In other words, a national satellite with the specific objective of bringing about socio-economic changes reached a vast section of rural population most of whom were never before exposed to any mass media or development message. The year-long experiment caught the attention of communicators and technologists all over the world. Its success virtually laid the foundation on which the entire plan of television expansion in the eighties was based. Following the SITE, the government of India accepted in principle that for domestic communication in the country, the satellite system was appropriate and should be developed.

During the period of SITE transmission, arrangement was made for regular feed back of viewers' reactions and information about reception conditions. Evaluation studies revealed the wide popularity of the SITE programmes. It was seen that illiterates learnt more from TV than the literates and the belief that educational programmes must be sugar-quote with lot of entertainment was not supported by survey findings. After SITE, women showed a greater gain in knowledge than men and a greater interest in family welfare matters, thus gradually reducing the knowledge gap. In primary school telecasts, there were significant gains in language development, listening comprehension and verbal fluency. There were also numerous instances of adoption of new agricultural, health, hygiene and family welfare practices. The SITE programmes also had a notable social impact. During community viewing people had to sit close together and caste distinctions tended to blur.

There were also some critical views about the SITE programme. Some considered that the experiment had been too expensive considering the likely benefit derived by the villagers. They argued that setting up ground TV stations instead would have yielded better results. Further, in matters like agriculture it was an unrealistic presumption that one common programme would meet the needs of the huge Hindi speaking states with wide variety of agro-climatic conditions. It was, however, conceded that one year was too brief a period to change any deep-rooted social practice. After the satellite facilities were withdrawn, Doordarshan setup six terrestoal transmitters at Raipur, Jaipur, Muzaffarpur, Gulbaraga, Hyderabad and Sambalpur in addition to the one at Pij to provide service to about 40 per cent of villages, originally covered by SITE.

Cable Television

In the mid-eighties, there was video. Today, cable TV is evoking the same interest and excitement in India. Cable television, originally called Community Antenna Television (CATV) developed initially in 1949 in the United States as a direct result of the limitations of broadcast television in reaching beyond the big cities where the TV stations were located. It, therefore, started as a mere extension of the nearby TV stations. Cable TV was introduced on an experimental basis for internal communication in Rourkela, by the Steel Authority of India first in 1982. Later, similar facilities were extended to Durgapur, Salem and Ranchi with increasing emphasis on employee participation. But today, the cable system has grown beyond recognition to bring its subscribers new services and countless channels that were undreamed of in the beginning. Besides local and distant broadcast stations, the cable system can provide the subscriber with satellite networks, microwave networks, automated channels, two-way interactive channels, local origination channels and all the programming associated with each other.

A cable TV system is basically an electronic distribution system that uses a master or dish antenna to receive an electronic signal and distribute it to subscribers over a cable strung throughout the city. It is a system through which signals from one source are transmitted to a number of TV sets through co-axial cables. The cables of a cable TV network are not meant to cross a public road unless specific licences have been obtained from the ministry of communications.

But then, of the 37,000 dish antennae in existence in India about 500 are C-band antennae which means they can receive foreign telecasts while the law says that only Doordarshan programmes can be received by dish antennae.

Cable TV has literally brought the world to our parlour and made a viewer truly an international citizen without any frontiers. Sitting in a remote corner in India, one had been able to experience all the horrors of the Gulf war beamed by the Cable News Network (CNN), the 24-hour global television news and feature service. Besides, the viewers can also tune in to Worldnet, Arabsat, Intelsat, BBC sports, Japansat and TV stations in China, the USSR, Saudi Arabia, Pakistan, Singapore and HongKong, thanks to the dish antennae of the cable operators.

Besides, an operator with a dish antenna can set up a control room and relay programmes on cable TV, providing an alternative channel to the subscribers. An operator sets up a dish antenna with the ostensible objective of catching Doordarshan programmes more clearly. However, a VCR is also connected and a cable TV network is born. The emphasis in India, is of course, predominantly on entertainment although during the Gulf war and such fast-breaking events, there was high premium on news and necessarily, its dramatic presentation. In fact, it was in exhilarating experience for many to see the battle of the Gulf raging tight inside their drawing room.

There has been a phenomenal explosion in the cable TV network since 1983-84 when the first cable TV outfit started operating in a handful of posh localities in south Bombay. But it never really took off. Because, while the installation of cable TV does not violate any laws (as long as it does not cross any municipal roads),what impeded its growth was the lack of software. Video copyright holders of films simply refused to part with the copyright of Hindi feature films for cable TV. The fear of being raided by INFACT(Indian Federation Against Copyright Theft) too was, therefore, a constant one. But after a prolonged legal battle, the major video copyright holders of feature films offered to give their cassettes to cable TV operator for a fee, from May 1, 1990. With this major road block demolished, cable TV started mushrooming all over the county.

The growth of cable TV is directly related to the inadequacies of Doordarshan programmes-the same factor behind the mushrooming of video magazines. Doordarshan is no longer being accepted as the primary source of TV viewing and its role may be further marginalized unless it breathes a new air of vitality in all its programmes. Another reason for this growth is that cost has been steadily coming down. Cable TV had emerged as an important medium for advertisement as well. A 10-second slot in Doordarshan costs a mind-boggling Rs 90,000 while in cable TV it is less than Rs 2000. It has one important advantage over video. An advertisement on a video film can be skipped by the in-built fast-forward mechanism. In a cable TV, a viewer has no such choice. Therefore, advertisers derive full value for money. Apart from entertainment, use of cable TV in education is unlimited. Once the proper educational software is developed, cable TV can carry it to every class room, thus giving a much needed boost to education. The roles of satellite television and cable TV are mutually complementary and not contradictory. Satellites serve as an efficient nation wide TV programme, bulk distributor to various cable networks. Cable network can carry among other things, programmes from several satellites onto individual TV sets.

The Indian population today receives indifferent quality of programme reception. Moreover, the single channel offered today beyond the four metropolitan cities, is totally inadequate if we wish to exploit this communication media and extend it to local language entertainment and education.

Programmes providing city level information are also vital to handle local community issues and add to local administrative and societal efficiency and convenience. People welcome cable as it offers increased choice. So far, networks like CNN have been only too glad to see their telecasts picked up in India, if only because viewership in this country is still small and CNN wants to build up a sizeable network of viewers. However, if Indian membership soars to a million, the expectation is that CNN would be interested in talking about royalties.

But how will the Indian government respond to the growth of cable TV and the use of dish antenna? Licence fees are perhaps to be hiked considerably. But controlling the use of antennae is a difficult proposition. The ethics of viewing cigarette and liquor advertisements will be debated afresh as more foreign programmes are watched by Indians. What about the dilemma of censoring TV programmes considered anti-national or provocative and anti-India slant in the news, if any? More serious questions however, still remain to be answered. Will it not further promote cultural rootlessness with constant exposure to alien values and settings? Can this become a national addiction as dangerous as the drugs, bringing in total degeneration and decadence? Will this turn us into "videots" as a nation? How is the society going to be affected in the long run? Can this pave the way for a kind of social colonialism?

An Information and Broadcasting Ministry Report on cable TV, submitted in June, 1991, recognised satellite communication as a new form of information dissemination that had broken national boundaries. But as an insurance against exposing the viewers to foreign perception and alien social values, the report recommended improving Doordarshan programmes to sustain the interest of viewers in a highly competitive field. The Committee agreed that control was essential regarding reception of foreign television signals. But it did not favour a total ban or absolutely free licensing of dish antenna systems.

The committee recommended setting up of a national cable authority to provide licence and regulate the growth of cable TV in the country. The report, submitted by an inter-departmental committee on cable television networks and dish antenna after devising an appropriate regulatory mechanism to cover their operation, both within private premises and across public property. A ban, the committee thought, would be "impractical" in view of its coming to stay in the country and a carefully regulated framework was essential in the contest of the disinformation possible through this network. The report made wide ranging recommendations on the subject with a clear distinction between cable TV networks with and without dish antenna and recommended prior approval from the Central Board of Film Certification before distribution of programmes through such networks and exhibition of feature film programme for copyright.

Television in Rural and Urban India

Indian television is the opposition between educational and entertainment programmes and its relation with the rural-urban dichotomy in India. This contradiction had its roots in the way television was conceived in India , and the ways in which policy questions were answered by early proponents of State-owned television. Education-via-television suggested a democratic and well distributed form of education, where television becomes a channel to disseminate the educational message to places where it is difficult to put up schools or provide teachers – mainly the rural sectors of India .This resulted in the linkage between education on television with a necessarily rural manifestation of this form of programming.

Television was introduced in 1959, when the first State sponsored experimental television broadcasts were beamed from the nation's capital, New Delhi. The biweekly , short broadcasts were primarily educational in nature , and only served a limited community within a 12 -15 mile radius of the transmission tower. Here in lay the beginning of the rural-urban tension, The transmitting center was in a major urban city , but the purpose of the broadcast was to benefit the rural communities around New Delhi. The material of broadcasts was tailored to suit the objective of imparting social and agricultural education (Dua, 1979). As Luthra (1986) has also pointed out, the programming included 'educative programmes about health , sanitation ,medical care, family planning and improved techniques of farming and agriculture', meanwhile , the urban-rural dichotomy was getting increasingly problematised as the education programmes started to include subjects that were not only of interest to the farming community but could also be of use to school children both in the cities and villages. This spilt was, therefore, not an even binary one between rural – education and urban-entertainment. This indicated that television could not remain as a medium that would be of interest to only a rural culture but would begin to interact with the urban culture too. This was formalized by the introduction of educational programmes for children in both rural and urban schools.

The wider scope of educational television was established on 23rd October 1961, with the formal setting up of the school and educational television system. Following this , a Committee of experts was appointed to study the status of television in India , compare it with other countries , and propose a set of directives to chart the development of television in India. The two key theoretical positions that informed this Commission were a trust in a model of Communication that suggested a linear flow of messages from an organized source to an anonymous audience and , secondly , a strong commitment to developmental television as an educational artifact.

The Commisssion , named the Chanda Commission(1966), evaluated the work being done by the various media units of the ministry of Information and Broadcasting. In their report , the Committee submitted a study of the development of television in India and suggested some strategies for development . Among the highlights of the report were the clear educational and instructional thrusts of television. The Commission concluded that television was conceived as a vehicle to help 'Illuminate' the masses about issues that were key concerns of the government. A matter of crucial importance was developing better methods of crop production, and informing the farmers of these methods. In the absence of an elaborate agricultural training infrastructure, television was considered to be an ideal solution. In addition, population control through the effective diffusion of information on birth control and family planning held a top position on the agenda. The Chanda Commission proposed:

1. A daily school service for all middle and higher secondary schools;
2. In - service training for school teachers and village level workers suitably adjusted to the differing needs of each state;
3. A daily programme for agricultural workers , for which all relevant information and guidance would be provided for the rural community on agricultural matters, interspersed with light entertainment to hold the attention of the viewers;
4. A daily social education service which would include literacy lessons, programmes for women , information and entertainment suitable for semi – educated and illiterate adults; and
5. Programmes for children (Government of India,1966).

For the Committee, the focus was on education, agriculture and the development of the rural sector. Consequently, educational television became the centre around which most media research developed. Educational television research also reiterated the necessary linkages between villages and educational television partly ignoring the urban manifestations of television. Yet the role of television in the urban areas remained a key issue, particularly because of the increase in entertainment programmes on television primarily directed towards the urban viewers.

The tension between education and entertainment was established at the very start of television in 1959. Exhibiting an indecision about the format and purpose of television , the initial programmes also included a fair amount of programming that was considered to be 'entertainment'. Luthra points out that soon after the experimental short broadcasts proved to be a technological success, the duration of broadcast was expanded to a ninety minute slot where 'entertainment fare, including music, dance and plays added in a large measure to the educative programmes (Luthra,H.R.,1986).There was a recognition that television could not remain just a channel for education but would include entertainment, although it was always made clear that entertainment would be the second priority . This is also highlighted in the Chanda Commission of 1964 which added a last item in their recommendation calling it 'programmes of entertainment'

Programmes for entertainment held a very low priority for the early planners. This was based on the view held by some policy makers that television entertainment necessarily portrayed low humor and exposed the seamier side of life. This is evident from the negative proclamation about entertainment, for instance , undoubtedly, constant exposure to television programmes portraying violence, the seamy side of life and degrading characteristics of human nature have a harmful effect on impressionable minds. Therefore, there was always an argument for 'attractive light entertainment' in good taste' and 'using the powerful medium of television for nation-building activities'. Common apprehensions existed that television would follow a path similar to the entertainment television of the West, particularly the US. There was also a large body of research available in the West, for instance the work of Gerbner(1970), that was establishing a direct linkage between social behaviour (live violence) in society and its depiction on television.

In spite of the assertion that education was primary, the strain between education and entertainment continued to increase. This was mainly due to the acquisition of better broadcasting technology , the proliferation of transmission centers and the lengthening duration of broadcasts. It was evident that more of entertainment was needed to fill up air time. Due to primitive indigenous production facilities, the source of entertainment programmes remained largely, in feature films and film-based programmes, imported foreign programmes, some appropriations from traditional mass Communication and sports.

By 1976, seven major cities (including Calcutta, Bombay, Madras and Jalandhar) had their own broadcasting facilities, with relay stations in various other cities. Each broadcasting centre had its own programming mixture, while remaining within the programme guidelines provided by the government. In 1979, Delhi television had a mix of programmes that included news, instructional programmes for children, women, farmers and in-service people. Entertainment programmes included feature film broadcast on weekends, film-based musical programmes, imported serials and the occasional airing of movies serial. Imported serials and the occasional airing of movie serials underscore the increasing urban orientation of entertainment television.

English is more readily understood by the more educated urban middle class audience.This was also the audience who were more exposed, primarily through western cinema, to the popular culture of the west. The imported programmes were closer in cultural proximity to the popular culture of educated urban India than rural India . Increasingly , there was a recognition that the imported English language programmes were meant for the privileged urban audience. Imported programmes included both entertainment and educational / instructional progammes which came mostly from the BBC and Russian television, and occasionally from the Unites States Information Services and the Canadian Broadcasting Corporation – all in English.

Another class of programmes included quiz and literary programmes. These programmes attempted to bring about a marriage between entertainment and instruction by presenting a quiz programme, often in English, moderates by a notable media personality. The language of broadcast usually included the local language and English. This was in keeping with the Chanda Commission recommendation that 'the language of television programmes must be that which isused in a particular region'.

Simultaneously, there was also a growing awareness that television was becoming an increasingly urban phenomenon. This was partly aided by the fact that the primary transmission centres were located in urban areas, and the urban middle class population had the material resources to buy receivers more readily than the rural viewers. While the rural viewers were largely dependent on community television sets, urban middle class viewers watched television on personal sets in the comfort of their homes.

Television was becoming increasingly accessible, particularly to the affluent urban groups who could afford private receivers . This meant that television was getting incorporated within the urban audience , who were beginning to link the practice of watching television with other social, cultural and domestic activities. In this sense, television was becoming a part if domestic everyday way of life – a part of urban culture. On the other hand, in the rural sector, television viewing was still largely a community affairs.

Indian Television – Doordarshan

Indian Television has changed a lot in the last few years in terms of programmes. The Doordarshan has realized the threat posed by cable and satellite TV which have entered in to the Indian Sub- Continent and pose a serious threat to Doordardhan in terms of viewership and this has made Doordarshan to change its outlook to the audience and had brought about a responsibility among the policy makers of Doordarshan . The advertisers of Doordarshan have more expectations from the programmes of Doordarshan so that their money is not merely spent on advertising in Doordarshan bring audiences to them and these audience would watch their advertisement regularly. This is also a factor in the changing trends of Indian television. The policy makers in the Government have realized that Doordarshan can be put to a better use, if it serves the development need of the government in reaching the people effectively. This is apparent because till today, Doordarshan is government owned in India and has responsibility to the audience in terms of fulfilling the development needs of the public.

The television medium is a part and parcel of the society on which it belongs and from where it function. In India, Doordarshan rightly belongs to the Indian society and it rightly reflects the values of the society is vast and composed of various segments and Doordarshan should reflect the values of the society. Sociologists and others say that the social values are bound to undergo changes from time to time and this should be reflected by the television medium, being a major medium of the Indian mass media. TV should not only reflect the values of the society but also should shape up these values as well. The responsibility of television at the turn of the 21st century is to prepare us to face the challenges of life in the technology, science, environment, population explosion and culture. All these should be made clear to the policy makers of Doordarshan, scientists, technologists, environmentalists, sociologists, psychologists and others.

As a principle mass medium owned by the government, Doordarshan has a major responsibility to face the challenges that is ahead and should provide suitable solutions to these problems.

1. Doordarshan, first of all should provide information to the people on various events happening around the country.
2. Doordarshan should also provide entertainment to the masses.
3. Doordarshan should serve as a medium of education and enlightenment.
4. Doordarshan should persuade people to participate in national integration schemes.
5. Doordarshan should promote Arts, culture, music, dance of people of different regions of the country.
6. Doordarshan should instill patriotism among the citizens by broadcasting programmes on national leader and their sacrifice made in the independent struggle.
7. Doordaeshan should organize programmes for children to promote education.
8. Doordarshan should aid and assist programmes in seeking public co – operation like;

(a) Family Planning programme,

(b) Rural Development programme,

(c) Adult education and eradication of illiteracy,

(d) Eradication of casteism, communalism and social evils etc.

9. Doordarshan as a principal mass medium in the country should organize programmes on various people belonging to various walks of life in order to fulfill their aspirations.

In the days that are ahead, we look forward to more number of programmes from Doordarshan on the positive aspects of the society in highlighting problems of under developed regions so that they can be brought to the attention of the public, policy makers and others.

The invasion of foreign satellite television, the government of India has starts a few channels in the Indian satellite system. These channels include, Metro channel, Entertainment and cultural channel, Sports channel and News and Current Affairs channel.

India has been experiencing a satellite TV revolution. From 1992 and even earlier the satellite Asiasat has beaming TV programmes to the millions in India. The popular satellite programmes that have come to the country are; Star TV, Zee TV, ANT, CNN, BBC, etc. All these satellite TV have been making tremendous impact in the lives of Indian citizens. Apart from these Channels, the popular Music Television has also come in to the country (MTV) and is viewed by the millions of Indian youth.

The cultural impact of these satellite TV on people has been enormous. A number of studies have been done to find out the impact of satellite TV on Indian public. The studies shows that the people are motivated by these foreign satellite

TV programmes and they are learning the cultural values of the western countries primarily that of the United States. The government of India is no doubt concerned about the cable TV but do not know how to go about the growing western influence on the Indian masses. In order to counter these influence the Government as already revamped in Doordarshan programmes and has started highly entertainment oriented Metro Channel. At present there is no action to stop the foreign satellite transmissions but countering these with that of Indian programmes launched from Indian satellite, i.e., the INSAT system.

The use and application of satellite TV in the country is not new. India has already used the AT-S-6 in 1975 when it conducted the SITE (Satellite Instructional Television Experiment) 2400 villages have been covered using the NASA Satellite in the six states of Andhra Pradesh, Bihar, Karnataka, Madhya Pradesh and Orissa. Everyday four hours of TV programmes were provided covering various aspects such as education, agriculture and family planning. But, what we have now is quite different from that of the SITE programme which was launched in 1975. Now, we have more of entertainment oriented programmes than educational or development oriented programmes.

Participating in a seminar that was held in Nov, 1992 on satellite and cable TV, the then minister of state for information and Broadcasting Mr. Ajit Kumar Panja said it is neither desirable nor feasible to stop these transmission or ban. No country can afford to sit back positively and let some foreign media decides what kind of programmes should be broadcast to the people of the country. It is only the viewing public can exercise choice and restraint. He continued that it is up to the media men in the country who can respond to the challenges and opportunities for open sky television affairs.

The Government can bring about comprehensive regulation and restriction binding the satellite TV industry.

As far as people are concerned, they should exercise their choice to see programmes that worth seeing. The satellite TV operators should broadcast programmes which are not alien to the local people and which will go into meeting the developmental task of the people who are concerned. There is a need for co-operation among the government, the satellite TV operators and the public, in evolving a comprehensive policy which would be satisfactory to all those who are concerned with satellite TV in this country.

3

Review of Literature

It is worthwhile for an investigator to make a comprehensive survey of what has already been done on the problem and its related aspects. Mouly (1964) therefore says, "survey of related literature avoids the risk of duplication, provides theories, ideas, explanations or hypotheses valuable in formulating the problem and contributes to the general scholarship of the investigators." The importance of related literature can not denied in any research because it is an important aspect of the research project.

Zuckerman, Singer and Singer conducted a study on the relationship between children's television viewing and their reading ability, reading habits and school behaviour. The children in the study were third, fourth and fifth graders, enrolled at two public schools in a middle-class suburb of New Haven, connectieut. The children were above average in terms of IQ and reading scores. The mean IQ was 110 on the McGraw-Hill IQ test, as compared to the national norm of 100 (Zuckerman, D.M., Singer, D.G., and Singer, J.L., 1980).

Ahmad in his study on effect of television of study hours of Pakistani Children, interviewed 94 television and 50 non-television children, 7-15 years old. Results show that television subjects studied at home for shorter hours than non-television subjects and that television subjects, only completed their school homework, in contrast to non-television subjects who devoted more time on school homework and self-study (Ahmad, A., 1980).

Gunter in the article "does television interfere with reading development," reviews evidence on the negative effects of television on reading development and examines the medium's potential as an instrument for positive attitude towards reading and academic work. Research has shown that television viewing not only affects academic efforts, but may also have a profound effect on cognitive development with serious implications for the child's ability to learn effectively in formal educational settings (Gunter, B., 1982).

Singer and Singer examined some of the ways television may influence the imagination, motor activity and aggressiveness of pre-school and early school-aged children. A model is proposed in which family and personal variables influence the growing child's response to television. On the basis of the results of empirical studies that investigated family influences, it is concluded that television may contribute to children's restlessness, dysphoria, fears about daily dangers and their proneness to aggression (Singer, J.L. and Singer, D.G., 1986).

Rubinstein in reviewing the book on "Television and social behaviour; beyond violence and children", mentioned that content specific effects such as that of television violence are rarely as specific or undimensional as they initially seem. Not only do the viewers bring their own attitudes and beliefs to the process of viewing, but also there are other conditional processes which modify the nature of those effects. The context in which the viewing take place, the pre-disposition of the viewers and even the sex can modify the effects of television viewing (Rubinstein, E.A., 1981).

Breen and Cercoran using prespectives from traditional and contemporary disciplines discuss the universality of myth and its functions within the frame work of television citing examples from television news coverage and popular culture. It is suggested that television realism acts as a silent weapon in the extension of certain ideologies over all others sections of society (Breen, M. and Cercoran. F., 1983).

Kent conducted participant observation field work among families with and without television from three ethnic groups in the U.S.; Navajos, Mexican-Americans and Euro-Americans. Typical days in the live of these families are described, which illustrate the strong impact of television-viewing on the diversity of activities performed by the families and show that the families basic patterns of the use of space were not altered by television-viewing. Every family with television whatever the ethnic group, spent large amount of time watching it. Television-viewing was the dominating evening and night activity and it reduced the diversity of activities (Kent, S., 1985).

Vidya Sagar conducted a content analyses of Bombay television transmission from December 1 to 31, 1977. The analysis was done from two angles. Firstly, the programmes were assessed keeping in mind their audience-wise targets. The maximum time was allotted for general programmes with subjects ranging from cabbages to kings. This came to 74 percent of the total transmission during one month. Next came children's programmes with 13 percent of a months' transmission. The remaining time allotted was 4 percent for youth, 4 percent for women, 3 percent for rural audience and 2 percent for the industrial workers.

The second aspect on which the analysis made was the significance given to the regional language that makes the medium effective. The children's programme were made with a language break-up of 36 percent in English, 26 percent in Hindi, 30 percent in Marathi and 8 percent in Gujarati. As regards youth, English took 28 percent, Hindi 21 percent,

Marathi 37 percent and 14 percent in Gujarati. Women's programmes were 11 percent in English, 33 percent in Hindi and 57 percent in Marathi.

The investigator concludes that if television programmes are to be effective, instructive and informative, these imbalances have to be rectified. If television is a developing agent and not another entertainment medium like cinema, clite interests should be cut down. This needs a thorough change in the programme planning and need-based programmes for each target audience with regional language as the main channel of communication (Vidya Sagar, M., 1978).

Kunhi Krishnan, Director of Thiruvananthapuram Doordarshan, in his article on "The Impact of Television," viewed that no other medium or institution since pre-industrial religion has had a comparable influence on what people of a tribe, community or nation have learned, thought or done in common. He opined that television exerts considerable influence on the lives of children and inculcates positive attitudes, values and behaviour though only less than five percent of the total programmes aimed at them. He suggested that television is now one of the major institutions and the creative intent and design of the unplanned curricular messages to television should also be taught to children. If we fail to help children understand this medium and be wise consumers of it, we miss an excellent opportunity to capture the constructive social, education and recreational use of television. We also neglect our adult responsibility of socialising the young people of all classes to handle the audio-visual messages being presented about their culture and their role in it (Kunhi Krishna, K., 1990).

Suriakanthi and Meenakshi conducted a study to survey the views of parents on the advantages and disadvantages of television watching by children, the optional time to be spent on television programmes suitable for children and suggestions towards minimising the ill effects of television on children (Suriakanthi, A. and Meenakshi, D., 1989).

Schramm and Parker expressed that there is something beyond age, intelligence and family which was affecting the children's viewing patterns. They believed that the missing elements were the child's social relations and some of his or her personal characteristics. So there is a need to first identify the important behavioural components of television viewing patterns, and to determine how these components contribute to personal and educational development as indicated by their adjustments to family, friends, daily routine activities and scholastic performance. It is possible that all these things are inter-dependent and what ultimately matters may be a complex set of inter-related variables (Schramm, W. Lyle, J. and Parker, E., 1961).

Maccoby in her study on "Television: Its impact on school children," interviewed 332 mothers of school children in the city of Cambridge, Massachusetts. She found the parents' attitudes toward television. A large majority say that if they were faced with the choice again of using their money for a television set or buying something, they would choose television. When asked specifically to name the disadvantages of television for a family with children, most owners were not able to think of a single disadvantage (Maccoby, E.E., 1951).

Bearling and Fullagar assessed children's attitudes to television advertisements. Five hundreds and forty-five middle-class white boys and girls completed a 28-item scale after viewing a television commercial. Initial analysis resulted in one item being omitted. Factor analysis of the remaining 27 items yielded two interpretable factors labelled entertainment and irritation-boredom. Two issues emerge-first children's and adult's attitudes to television advertisements differ some what. Second children view television advertisement almost entirely in terms of their entertainment function (Barling, J. and Fullagar, C., 1983).

Bouchalova, observed socio-economic changes in families that occured during the 1st 6 years of their child's life. Analysis indicated that the family's social background affected the children's school achievement and least obvious in average school grades. The greatest influence on children's scholastic success was exerted by parental education level, the least by housing conditions. Changes were greater in boys than girls (Bouchalova, M. et al., 1981).

Narayan conducted a study on the "Impact of Television on Viewers". The study sample consists 300 families having television in Bombay city, chosen by random sampling method. The actual collection of data of the haousehold and the viewers reaction was through questionnares containing both multiple choice questions and a qualitative nature. Most of the viewers in the sample in Bombay city belonged predominantly to the middle income group, were aged between 35 to 45 years and included a large proportion of house-wives and retired persons. The viewers were asked if they had the habit of visiting their friends before they had acquired the television sets and if they continued this habit after they had purchased television sets. This was done to ascertain if television viewing affected family togetherness and reduced sacialibility. On an analyse of the answers, it appears that there was a distinct relationship between television viewing and sociability (Narayan, A., 1987).

Gaddy studied the relationship between television use and academic achievement using data from the high school and beyond study by S.S. Peng et al., (1981). It was hypothesised that, for high school students as a group, television-viewing leads to lower achievement. Among the measures in the survey are tests of academic achievement, measures of leisure time use and an assortment of indicators of personal and social context. The analysis technique used was liner structural modeling of 2-wave panel data. Results clearly replicate the consistent finding of past studies a uniform and highly significant negative correlation between television and achievement (Gaddy, G.D., 1986).

Comstock examined the impact of television on American institutions. According to him television's presence in the American home has brought many changes in family life and the rearing of children, including new patterns of interaction, alteration of activities and vicarious socialization. The most obvious effect of television is the introduction of a variety of images, statements and potrayals in to the home. One strand of this evidence is the amount that children view and the content itself. Comstock opined that children typically are heavy viewers, and most of their viewing is of general audience or adult programming: the average of children of elementary school age is 27 hours per week. Television presents the viewers with a world that often is at variance with one he/she inhabits. This is particularly so far children, whose experience and knowledge are limited. Thus what television conveys often has no corrective in actual experience (Comstock, G., 1978).

Tangney examined the relations of children's television content preference to children's perceptions of parent-child conflict and parents' child-rearing attitudes. Subjects were white male and female students from a large Los Angeles public elementary school. Data from 165, fourth-fifth and sixt-grades students were collected. Questionnares accompanied by a letter briefly explaining the focus of the study were sent to parents who provided addresses on their child's permission form. These questionnaries included the adult/adolescent parenting inventory, a section on parental supervision of children's television-viewing and demographic information (Tangney, J.P., 1988).

Tucker studied the extent to which light, moderate and heavy television viewing related to multiple measures of obesity and physical fitness among 379 males (mean age 15.7 years). Light television viewers scored significantly better than heavy viewers in a composite fitness and on pushups, pullups, side step, situps and jog-walk considered individually. Light viewers on the composite fitness measure and on pushups, pullups and jog-walk. Light viewers displayed a strong but insignificant tendency toward better fitness, than moderate viewers on long jumps, situps and side-step tests. Light viewers were not significantly less obese than moderate or heavy viewers. It is concluded that for purposes of good physical fitness, television-viewing should be limited to one hour or less per day (Tucker, L.A., 1986).

Ribeiro de Almeida and Aparccido do Silva, studied the pre-dilection and habits of Brazilian children that watch television. The sample was composed of 145 families. A questionnaire was used to investigate the following topics: educational level of parents, daily time period that subjects prefer to watch television, type of programmes they prefer and other activities in which subjects participate. Results indicate that subjects watched television for about 4 hours per day and preferred 12-6 p.m. for their viewing period. Comedies, adventure stories, violent moves and soap operas were the preferred programmes (Rebeiro de Almedia, A. and Aparcido de Silvia, J., 1982).

Buerkel, investigated the relationship between children's exposure to television potrayals of communication behaviour among family members and their expectations about the real life occurence of such behaviour in family settings. Television content, children's perceptions, parental questionnaire responses of 648, 4th-8th graders. Results indicate that children who frequently watch family show appear to believe that families in real life show support and concern for each other. Parents positive interventions, such as guiding their children toward family shows, viewing with them, commenting on show content and maintaining control over the amount of viewing, can enhance what children learn about affiliative behaviour from viewing family television shows, parental guidance also can limit learning about non-affiliative behaviour from television families (Buerkel, R., et al., 1982).

Maniar studied the influence of television viewing on adolescents, which threw light on the positive side of television. The findings revealed high influence on development of civic competence and moderate influence on other development tasks such as body image, sex roles, independence, future roles, preparation for family life and preparation for career. Television viewing facilitated their discussions on sex matters and understanding of the changes occurring in their body (Maniar, A., 1994).

Nathani (1986) found that television viewing motivated adolescents to participate in sports, drama, music and adventurous activities. Mahajan (1988) found that television helped people in increasing their familiarity with different religions.

Eashwar studied the impact of cable TV on women in terms of activities, time management and interactions with family members and the outside world. Findings of the study revealed that cable TV did have a profound effect on the activities of women. It increases considerably the isolation of women by restricting her interactions with the husband, children, other members of the family, friends and neighbours. This happens both due to her own involvement with the TV, as well as the involvement of the other members of the family, in watching the cable TV and regular TV programmes (Eashwar, L., 1994).

A study by Mahajan on "the case of Television in India" revealed three basic behavioural characteristics regarding the televiewing by the young Indian women. First, they are frequently watching television programmes. Secondly, they on an average devote one to three hours daily to televiewing. Thirdly, they want television for the purpose of recreation rather than education or information to a great extent (Mahajan, K., 1993).

Bhatia studied the influence of TV advertisements on adolescents of Baroda city. She found moderate impact of TV advertisements on their physical, social, emotional and cognitive development as well as on relationship with their parents. Adolescent were highly influenced by TV advertisements in adopting the ways of expressing one's self. They developed liking for a well decorated home by viewing TV advertisements. They enjoyed seeing their favourite models and sportsman in the advertisements and they expressed that they wanted to become like them. Their general knowledge also increased and they developed ability to differentiate between the different brands of the same products. Some of them understood the motive behind the TV advertisement (Bhatia, R., 1997).

Chatterjee in his book examines the historical growth of TV in India. Later on he passes on to discuss the implications. According to the author, the emergence of TV has posed a serious threat both to radio and cinema. The TV has also effected the press in advanced countries. It is replacing morning newspaper in many homes and the press is gradually moving further into the area of comments and features (Chatterjee, R.K., 1973).

Bhattacharya has studied the role of the Satellites communication in telecasting the TV programmes. He analysed the role of TV at the national and international levels. According to him the people of the world which are facing conflict and dispute, tension and turmoil, stress and strain can come under the common umbrella with the help of mass telecasts transmitted by the Satellites. The Satellites communication has opened the new possibilities for the different nations to cooperate for the common cause of removing poverty and improving relations among all the nations. It can also help in bringing about social and the political consciousness amongst the masses of the developing countries (Bhattacharya, V.R., 1976).

Agarwal made a social evaluation of SITE programmes in rural Gujarat which has come to be known a kheda study. The authors observed that the TV programmes on agriculture, animal husbandary and poultry raised the level of awareness of the people. It evoked in them the desire to do new things and the demand for the availability of infrastructure which they could use for their development. The author also observed that the TV provoked empathy and sense of efficiency among the viewers (Agarwal, B., 1986).

Lowry studied the way the TV programmes influence alcohol consumption pattern. The author found that the prime-time TV net work programmes encourage rather than discourage alcohol consumption pattern. The TV network have had to make use of alcohol by keeping in view the success of their programmes than the welfare of the society (Lowry, D.T., 1981).

Riju carried out a study to test the notion whether the local television newscast a stress local public affairs or emphasize sensationalism or human interest stories. The author found that this notion to a great extent was valid but qualified it by saying that the critical test of selecting news stories is not whether they belong to public affairs or sensationalism but to their appeal to the audience's immediate concern (Riju, J.S., 1982).

Tan and Kinner made a study to find out the way the social interaction of the children is influenced by the TV programmes. The authors suggest that the children who saw a particular episode were found to engage in friendly social interaction with the white children compared to those who were not shown this programme (Tan, A.S., and Kinner, D., 1982).

Gantz and Zohoori wanted to examine the effects of television on individual's living patterns. As the authors formulate the problem "Are lives restructured to accommodate television or is television fit into the structure of daily life"? the authors examined for this study purpose the evening TV viewing and bed time patterns preceding and following Indian's one hour evening schedule shifts. The authors found out the functional relationship between television schedules and the audience behaviour. The authors maintain that most of the respondents were willing to structure their lives around their television (Gantz, W., and Zohoori, A.R., 1982).

Johnson conducted a study on English and Australian youths to find out the role of TV in their lives. The author argues that it is not the content that is central to the social role of TV but the 'form and the mode of operation'. The youths were found to make different uses of the TV programmes according to their respective cultures. The findings suggest that this difference can be explained in terms of the relationship between the culture of home and school. For those whose home and school culture were roughly the same, they treated TV viewing as a cultural exercise. On the otherhand, for those youths whose home culture differed markedly from school culture, they treated the TV viewing as providing a set of themes which they could use to resist the school culture and also to reflect its legitimacy (Johnson, L., 1984).

Desai in his study on social context and value system puts forward to suggestion that if the TV programmes have to be successful; they have to operate in the social context of the value system of the people. The television programmes therefore should incorporate the diverse heritage of our country in arts, crafts, music, dance and languages so that they become understandable to the masses of India (Desai, M.V., 1986)

Kishore in his study has suggested that the cable TV connections have provided more advantage to the urban population as compared to the rural masses due to the poor receiving of the TV programme (Kishore, K., 1994). Rao and Raghavan suggested that cable TV connections have provided more variety of information and entertainment programmes and hence the people feel attracted to the cable connections (Roa, N.B., and Raghavan, J., 2000). Saksena is of the opinion that the potential of television can be utilised for imparting education and information to the masses because in the next millennium traditional method would prove inadequate (Saksena, G., 2000).

Dutta is critical about the power of Television and observes that, "...the arrival of satellite channels with foreign commercial programming has not presented us with an alternative to the old discourse of power. Instead, our signification of the world beyond the box is now organised by information and images processed under political-economic conditions in which an Indian audience is irrelevant. In other words, the assumptions that form the televisual content of most satellite channels are part of a process of production tailored to meet the demands of advertisers and shareholders of another country. This does not neccessarily imply that we are being indoctrinated by malevolent foreign powers through Satellite Television in a high-tech "war of the world's scenario. It means, rather, that the media in question is more concerned with the business of ratings and corporate sponsorships." Dutta further argues, in the Satellite Television era, cold blue scrutiny has grown more powerful-till it invades almost every aspect of our thoughts and actions. Many a decision is made and opinion formed on the basis of what was seen on the BBC/Star Plus/CNN (Dutta, S., 1996).

Joshi of the Social Research Group in the Development and Educational Communication Unit of the Indian Space Research Organisation, Ahmedabad surveyed the media exposure of 400 persons in the age group 18-75 years to find out the perceptions of the respondents regarding the ethnic issues and the role played by different media in the reporting of the ethnic issues. The most positive role according to both students and non-students as well as all the religious groups in the sample was played by the English language newspapers. Doordarshan was ranked number two and regional newspapers were ranked three. Most studies in India point out that it is not Doordarshan, but the Cable Television which is largely responsible for a variety of distortions, including culture (Joshi, S.R., 1996).

Jha and Sinha have observed that Television was viewed by a majority of the audience as the medium of entertainment rather than education and information (Jha, R.C. and Sinha, B.P., 1980).

Chaudhury's doctoral study based on a survey of 100 schools from nine districts of the Rajasthan State, investigated into the attitude of the Television custodian teachers towards school Television, and examined the relationship between teacher's attitude on the one hand and their job satisfactory and mass media behaviour on the other hand. The results indicate an overall favorable correlation between teacher attitude and job satisfaction and between teacher attitude and mass media behaviour. One-third of the teachers in the sample schools were using Radio and Television as tools of teaching (Chaudhury, S.S., 1994).

Mehra's study of the Sociology of TV viewing behaviour indicated that illiterate, low-educated, middle aged respondents of nuclear families engaged in service were found to devote more time on an average per day on TV than others. Certainly foreign media, particularly the electronic media-cable TV- has its impact on Indian culture (Mehra, S., 1985). The impact can be both positive and negative. The positive impact lies in its utility to spread knowledge, promote awareness and breed understanding. The negative impact is usually highlighted in terms of corrosion of traditional values, cultural imperialism and orientation to sex, violence etc.

Gopal Saksena observes that the availability of multi-channels and multi-national Television in India has given rise to a much more discriminating, perceptive, demanding viewership. Instead of blaming it on the TV, it is for the viewers to be specific about their choices as different channels cater exclusively to different tastes and preferences. The viewers are not neccessarily dependent any longer on what the TV offers, but they can pick and choose what they want to view (Saksena, G., 1996).

Narayanan's doctoral study in Sociology which dealt with the TV viewing habits of children in Mumbai reveals that TV keeps children indoors in the evening when they should actually be engaged in vigorous outdoor play. Though TV is supposed to provide information and knowledge, Narayanan said few of his respondents reported that TV glued kids to get good grades in examinations (Narayanan, A., 1983).

Singh reviewed 108 published works on the impact of Television. Almost all of these focused on the impact on children and education, particularly in the context of rural India. Singh's broad conclusions are that TV has changed the habits of the children. Educational TV has a positive impact and helped children to gain more knowledge (Singh, R., 1992).

Unnikrishnan and Bajpai covered 730 children, some of their parents, teachers, experts and advertisers during their field work in Delhi and studied the extent to which advertising shapes the consciousness of children; what they are learning from Television; and whether television advertising is establishing a social and consumption agenda for children to follow. The study reveals the excitement and the confusion created in the minds of children by what they see on the small screen. It explains that the manner in which children negotiate TV information and advertising messages varies according to their socio-economic background (Unnikrishnan, N. and Bajpai, S., 1996).

Kalra and Kalra studied the impact of Cable TV viewing on adolescents. The study was conducted in four colonies of Ludhiana City in Punjab covering a sample of 150 adolescents in the age group 13-19 who had cable TV connections in their houses. The authors point out that the media invasion has triggered off a number of unhealthy trends in the society. It has even interfered with social mingling and family bonds. The 'Villain' has driven guests away and injected lethargy into the youth and students. Studies have gone out of gear and the ocular, physical and mental health of the 'victims' have been affected. The authors point to the special responsibility of the parents in curtailing the negative effects of Cable TV (Kalra, R.K. and Kalra, A., 1996).

Deodhar rightly summed up the dilemmas concerning the impact of TV: "TV is a double edged weapon. It can be the healing knife of a surgeon or the stabbing weapon of a killer". The book very aptly brings home the point that a child builds its character, its intelligence and its knowledge level in the constant company of its two parents, the mother and the father. Tele-video at home or at school or at the community place may soon become the third parent (Deodhar, P.S., 1991).

Ninan has reflected on the reactions of diverse groups of people to a variety of instances from TV shows and observes that, "The tension between TV depictions and their reception only reflected, in a sense, the contradictions in a rapidly changing Indian society, where new mores were emerging even as old values remained entrenched. And women, both on the box and in the home, were often at the centre of this uneasy co-existence" (Ninan, S., 1995).

Markandan observed that TV is not an unmixed blessing. According to him the problem is more with Cable TV that TV as such (Markandan, N., 1995). Bhattacharya documents how cinema lost the 'family audience' and TV quickly seized the opportunity and launched its own serials based on high voltage family melodrama. Her analysis is in the context of the United Nations declaring 1995 as the year of International Year of the family. Bhattacharya, however, questions the TV reinforcing the myth of the typical Indian family with male headed hierarchy as the normative model (Bhattacharya, R., 1995).

Collins conducted a questionnaire based study of about 300 secondary schools children in Northern Ireland to discover their viewing preferences. It was found that more than two-thirds had a TV sets in their rooms, that most of them were unconcerned about the level of violence on TV, and that they were attracted to situations and characters that were humorous rather than violent. Parents were reported as exerting little control over these young one's viewing (Collins, J., 1983).

Ray Brown has revealed that the information that we acquire from TV is not simply an acquaintance with current events, but is perhaps more a sort of 'reality orientation' in the adult world. The Television's contribution to this reality orientation has been shown to relate less to family and peers, with whom the child is in any way familiar and more to values and concepts concerning occupations, status and people's roles outsides the home and the school (Brown, R., 1976).

From the review of literature mentioned above admits that the Television has considerable power to influence beliefs and behaviour of the individuals in the society.

4

The Study Area–City of Shillong

Shillong is the capital of Meghalaya at an altitude of 1561 meter above the mean sea level. On its west and south lies the Bangladesh plain, to the west the Barak valley and to the north the valley of the Brahmaputra (Assam plain). The region enjoys a sub-tropical monsoon climate. The amount of rainfall within the region varies, ranging from between an average 300 to 400 cm, annually. Despite its undulating topography, the rejuvenated parts of the plateau leads to quick soil formation combined with high average annual rainfall that permits thick and quick vegetal growth.

Shillong is situated in the East Khasi Hills District and is linked by National Highway No.40 with the state capital Assam at a distance of 103 km. In the past it was a few cluster of scattered hamlets under the jurisdiction of the Syiem of Mylliem. Since the year 1866, Shillong became the provisional headquarters of the Khasi and Jaintia Hill districts. Again in 1874, Shillong was made the capital of the Assam province. Between 1905 to 1912 Shillong was turned into summer capital of newly created province of Eastern Bengal and Assam. Since then Shillong had remained the capital of

Assam. However, in 1972, Meghalaya attained its full statehood and Shillong became the capital of the state.

Legends say that in ancient times a man names "SHYLLONG" discovered a deity in the Shillong peak and, therefore, the place derived its name as "SHILLONG". Among the Khasi people many such legends are current. It has got a number of tiny tablelands sparse between small hillocks. Clear water oozes out from underground sources in several places. Besides there are some perennial rivulets flowing across the city, which provide very good habitation for men and animals. Quite a number of attractive waterfalls are located within and around the city, such as Bishop's Falls, Beadon Falls, Crinoline Falls, Sweet Falls, Spread Eagle Falls, Elephant Falls etc. The highest peak is said to be the Shillong peak with a height of 6445 ft. above mean sea level. Unlike many cities of India, the atmospheric air of Shillong remains free from dirt, soot's and smoke. Approximately the humming pine trees mix their gaseous aroma containing curative ingredients for some diseases with the gentle gales that blow through the pine – needles. Rain and showers with occasional hails are welcomed gifts of nature in automatic cleansing and washing out the dirt and dregs as well as in providing rain water for collection from the house tops by every needy person for ordinary house-hold uses. The climate is humid, healthy and salubriously agreeable throughout the year. During winter, the temperature comes below freezing point and snow-flakes and frosts appear to add to the joys and fun of the youngsters. To speculative minds, the Kaleidoscopic colour variations of the sky over heading Shillong are of absorbing interests.

The British pooled in as much resources as possible for developing and making this hill-town congenial and enjoyable to their modes of living as best as possible. The beautiful Wards Lake, Polo ground, the race-course, the Governor's residence, the link-roads connecting the neighboring plains, patronization of the Christian European missionaries with big grants of lands etc., of the establishment of quality hospitals, schools and colleges, churches and so forth are some of the good instances. They could easily discover and imagine with their world-wide experiences that Shillong was a potential virgin soil to model it into a QUEEN OF THE HILL-STATIONS on the one hand and their best stronghold in the EAST-INDIA for propagation of British power and culture. In such criss-cross pulls, anyhow Shillong has become the cleanliest, both naturally and artistically modernized, Queen of the cities of India.

Growth of Population

Shillong town is an overgrown village. The population of Shillong has increased at a rapid pace leading to acquisition of new settlements under urban areas. Similarly, the share of workers in traditional non primary occupation has declined to a great extent adding more to their existing urban characteristics.

Thus, in 1931, an Urban Agglomeration was formed in the state capital with Shillong municipality and Shillong cantonment as constituent units. In 1961, two more towns, viz. Nongthymmai and Mawlai were added and expanded the area of Shillong Urban Agglomeration (UA). In 1981, two more towns known as Pynthorumkhrah and Madanrting were added to the Shillong (UA). Thus, increasing the total number of the constituents units of Shillong (UA) to 6 numbers. There is no new town in 1991 census. In the 2001 census a new town known as Nongmynsong has come up and formed a new constituent units of Shillong (UA). Although 7 towns including Shillong municipality constitutes an Urban Agglomeration. The constituent towns are Mawlai, Nongthymmai, Madanrting, Pynthorumkhrah, Nongmynsong, Shillong (municipality) and Shillong cantonment. There is only one Urban Agglomeration with 7 constituent towns in the state in 2001. Shillong municipality is the core town of urban agglomeration. The total population of Shillong Urban Agglomeration is 2,67,881 person with 1,4,416 males and 1,33,465 females.

Table 4.1
Population Growth of Shillong Municipality

Year	*Persons*	*Decadal Variation(+)*	*Decadal Variation (P.C)*
1901	9621	—	—
1911	13639	+4018	+41.76
1921	17203	+3564	+26.13
1931	26536	+9333	+54.25
1941	38192	+11656	+43.93
1951	58512	+20320	+53.20
1961	72438	+13926	+20.80
1971	87659	+15221	+21.01
1981	109244	+21585	+24.62
1991	131719	+3894	+20.57
2001	132876	+19638	+0.88

Source : Census of India.

Table 4.1 shows the distribution and growth of population within Shillong municipality ward-wise. Population of Shillong municipality has grown from a mere 9,621 in 1901 to 1,31,719 in 1991, roughly 13 times in 90 years. This may look impressive but as events of last two decades indicate it is not as spectacular as witnessed in many similarly placed cities even within the region. One reason for this has been cited as under-reporting during the decadal censuses. The other is that largest part of the growth is accounted for in the adjacent townships and also areas that have became urbanized but are still classified as rural and are not included within the municipal jurisdictions.

The population of Shillong municipal area as on 1st March 2001, is 1,32,876 which is only 19,738 persons more than 1991 census having a growth rate of 0.88 percent during 1981- 1991 having more than 3.56 percent. The population of Shillong (M) as per 1991 census shows that the growth rate during the decade 1991-2001 is the lowest when compared with the earlier decades. In Shillong municipal area there is no further scope for expansion of residential housing pattern.

Population Growth of Shillong Urban Agglomeration

The population of Shillong (UA) as on 1st March 2001 is 26,7881 and the decadal growth rate during 1991-2001 is 19,93 percent. The growth rate of the State population of Meghalaya during the decade 2001 is only 29.49 percent, which is less by merely 3 percent from the last decade which was at 32.86 percent. East Khasi Hills Distrtict which is having the largest number of population among all the districts of the State with a population of 6,60,994 as per 2001 census, shows the lowest rate with 22.88 percent. On the other hand, Shillong (M) is the core town of Urban Agglomeration. The total population of Shillong (UA) for both males and females is 1,34,416 and 1,33,465 respectively. The comparative population growth of Shillong during 1991-2001 is shown in (table 4.2) below.

Sex Ratio of Shillong Urban Agglomeration

As per 2001 census, the sex ratio of the State is 975 as against 955 in 1991. Sex ratio has gradually declined over the decades. The gradual increase in the sex considerable improvement of the sex ratio has been noticed in census 2001 as compared to 1991 census. The decadal variation of sex ratio during 1991-2001 is highest in East Khasi Hills District.

While comparing the sex ratio of the different districts with that of the State sex ratio, East Khasi Hills has the highest sex ratio of the State average. Meghalaya is at rank 7 in terms of sex ratio among the Indian States with regards to Shillong (M) area the total number of females as per 2001 census is 66,747 and males is 66,129 in numbers. In Shillong Agglomeration the number of females is 1,33,464 and males 1,34,416 numbers. The difference of population by sex is 951. (Table 4.3) below shows the sex ratio of Shillong Urban Agglomeration.

Table 4.2
Comparative Population Growth of Shillong

City / District / State	*Population in Number 2001 -1991*	*Decadal Growth Rate 1991-2001-1981-91*		
1. Shillong (M)	1,32,876	1.30.691	0.88	+19.63
2. Shillong (U,A)	2,67,881	2,22,273	19.93	+27.23
3. East Khasi Hills Dist.	6,60,994	6,57,160	22.88	+28.50
4. Meghalaya	23,06,069	17,74,778	29.94	+31.80

Sources: Census of India.

Table 4.3
Sex Ratio of Shillong Urban Agglomeration

Name of U.A	1961	1971	1981	1991	2001
Shillong U.A	762	855	902	888	993
Mawlai	960	938	905	870	1,077
Nongthymmai	852	881	912	944	1,077
Madanrting	-	-	950	955	970
Shillong(M)	785	765	762	765	752
Shillong Cant.	466	765	762	765	752
Pynthorumkhrah	-	-	867	863	942
Nongmynsong	-	-	-	-	971

Sources: Census of India.

Present Trends

During the last three decades or so the city has undergone a radical transformation from a hill resort to a multifunctional service centre, catering to a host of administrative and other service functions not only for the State but for the entire North East Region, comparable next to Guwahati. From a small village in 1866 to a class-I city in 2001, the city has grown to cater to the needs of the state as an enclave of modernization in the midst of the rural –tribal hinterland that continued without any significant change. The modern transport network and expansion of the city infrastructure have influenced the tribal social order but only to a limited extent thereby giving rise to a dualistic economic organization.

Higher Education in Meghalaya

College and University Education in the State

Students of Meghalaya can take up their college studies after passing the higher secondary examination. There are fifty-two colleges affiliated under the only university in the state, the North Eastern Hill University (NEHU), Shillong, with two campuses in Shillong and another in Tura. The NEHU is a central university, set up by an Act of Parliament on 26 May 1973 and formally inaugurated on 19th July 1973 with the motto "Rise up and build". The objectives of the university are "to disseminate and advance knowledge by providing instructional and research facilities in such branches of learning as it may deem fit; to pay special attention to the improvement of the social and economic conditions and welfare of the people of the hill areas of the north –eastern region, and, in particular, their intellectual, academic and cultural advancement." The NEHU's jurisdiction initially extended to the states of Meghalaya, Nagaland and Mizoram, and had rather well established campuses in those two states as well, in Kohima and Medziphema in Nagaland and Aizawl in Mizoram. In 1979 the University had also taken over the Pachhunga Memorial Government College with the new name Pachhanga University College in Mizoram. With the establishment of two central teaching and affiliating universities in the states of Nagaland and Mizoram, (Nagaland University on 6th September 1994 and Mizoram University on 2nd July 2001) the NEHU's jurisdiction had ceased over them. The Tura campus became functional in 1996 with English and Garo departments to begin with. Today other departments in subjects like Rural Development, Horticulture and MBA are added to this campus.

The NEHU now has six schools, twenty-eight departments and four centers of studies. The prestigious Regional Sophisticated Instrumentation Centre (RSIC) funded by the Department of Science and Technology, Government of India, is being run at this university. Research programmes and projects in the university have been of high order, especially in departments like chemistry, botany, zoology, sociology and history. The university has been accorded a four-star status by the NAAC for a period of five years in September, 2000. Presently there are 53 under-graduate colleges which are affiliated under the NEHU. The North-East Regional Institute of Science and Technology (NERIST), situated in Itanagar, is also affiliated under NEHU. The NEHU Central Library boasts of about two lakhs books, thousands of bound periodicals,326 foreign subscriptions of journals of international repute and to 366 Indian journals. The students of the university have shown diligence in their studies and have marked excellent achievements in career.

Table 4.4 is the list of colleges in Shillong, which supply students for higher education. However, it should be noted that a sizeable number of students come also from other states of India and especially the north- east. Shillong has been a haven for higher education to the tribal students of Mizoram, Nagaland and, to some extent, Arunachal Pradesh ever since the beginning of higher education in this beautiful hill resort. Its salubrious climate and friendly atmosphere that existed before the xenophobic fears caught the local psyche and popular imagination, together with the existence of some leading colleges in the region like St. Edmund's, St. Mary's, St. Antony's, Lady Kean College and the UCC on the suburb of Shillong, have added to the rise of Shillong as an educational town. The hills tribals of the region prefer no better destination to continue their higher studies than Shillong.

Table- 4.4
List of Colleges in Shillong

Sl.No.	*Name of Institution / College*
1.	Synod College, Shillong
2.	Seng Khasi College, Shillong
3.	Buddha Bhanu Saraswati College,Shillong
4.	Shillong College, Shillong
5.	St. Edmund's College, Shillong
6.	Women's College, Shillong
7.	Bissau College, Shillong
8.	Morning Star College,Shillong
9.	Good Will College, Shillong
10.	St. Mary's College, Shillong
11.	Lady Keane College,Shillong
12.	Sankardev College, Shillong
13.	Raid Laban College, Shillong
14.	Shillong Commerce College, Shillong
15.	Umshyrpi College, Shillong
16.	Upper Shillong College,Shillong
17.	Greater Mawlai College,Shillong
18.	Alpine College, Shillong
19.	Nabon Synod College, Shillong
20.	St. Anthony's College, Shillong
21.	St. Dominic's College, Shillong
22.	Mawlai Presbyterian College, Shillong
23.	Christian Academy College, Shillong

Source – CDC, 2002, NEHU, Shillong.

Historical Background of Colleges in Shillong Under Study

St. Edmund's College

The first college of general education to be set up in any part of today's Meghalaya is St. Edmund's College, Shillong. The history of St, Edmund's College is intermingled with the brave efforts of the Germans and the Irish. St. Edmund's College was founded by the Irish Christian Brothers in the year 1916 as a higher secondary school and was recognized by the Cambridge University for examination up to Higher School Certificate level. Bro. Luke Aherne was the first director of St. Edmund's College and Bro. M. S. O'Brien, the first sub-director. St Edmund's College was officially opened on 6th October 1916 by the Chief Commissioner of Assam and an educationist, Sir Archdale Earle, with 32 boarders and 8 day scholars. The institution grew rapidly and by 1918 it had 89 boarders and 23 day scholars. A hospital was built in 1918 where now stands the Scholasticate. In 1919, the number increased to 100 boarders and 16 day scholars. Out of them, 8 boys were sent, for the first time, for Higher Cambridge Local Certificate Examinations and 3 passed. This was considered a remarkable achievement. Under the changed circumstances with the coming of Government of India Act,1919, the college was affiliated to Calcutta University for Intermediated Arts (I.A.) and Intermediate Science (I.Sc.) courses in 1923. In 1934-35, Bro. J.C. Roe conceived the idea of opening up University classes up to B. A. and B. T (Bachelor of Teaching) standards. Extension of affiliation to the B. A. and B.T standards was granted on 14th September 1935. This was the first time when a non-government college in the united Assam province got affiliation up to B.A. and B. T standards. With the birth of Guahati University in 1948, the college came to be affiliated under that university. The DPI of Assam and the guardian asked St. Edmund's College to open B. Sc. Classes in 1953 and the government wrote to the college officially for the same purpose in 1955. The science stream was thus started in August 1959. With the birth of the North-Eastern Hill University in 1973, the college came under that university. Bro. M.G. Shannon, the then principal of the College, nursed for more than 5 years a college for women which is now one of the leading colleges in Shillong (Women's college, Shillong) till it was shifted to its own premises in early 1990. St. Edmund's College did not lie on the laurels of its glorious past, but continuously strove to introduce new streams and courses. Thus the commerce stream came in 1997, the Department of Biochemistry at degree pass and honours level followed suit and the college authorities decided to admit female students to degree and honours level. In St. Edmund's College, this state had the right pioneer of higher education. In matters of excellence and commitment, St. Edmund's has not lagged behind; it still is one of the outstanding colleges in the whole of north-eastern region. Only recently has the college been able to be accessible to the common man. Previously it remained rather elitist, meant largely for selected few. In 2007, two more new departments opened i.e., Social Work and Environmental Science in the College.

St. Anthony's College

The St. Anthony's College, Shillong, was the second institution of higher education in today's Meghalaya established and managed by the Catholic educational society, namely, the Salesians of Don Bosco. Guided by the educational philosophy of St. John Bosco, the college was founded in 1934 to bring college education within the reach of the common man. Ever since, St. Anthony's has been in the vanguard of higher education in north-east India and had been recognized as one among the leading colleges in the country by the UGC. The college was successively affiliated to the Calcutta, Guahati and North-Eastern Hill Universities. In tune with the developments in educational strategies worldwide, the college has pioneered courses in application-oriented subjects like biotechnology, computer science, mass communication and video production, pisciculture, business administration, biochemistry, media technologies etc. to answer to the needs of the community that it serves and to give its graduates a competitive edge in the employment market. Student development services department (career guidance, personal counselling and coaching for entrance examinations) is the latest venture of the college to position its student right at the heart of its life and activity. The college opted for accreditation by the NAAC in pursuance of its quality enhancement strategies and was declared accredited with a five star status in September 2000, being the first and the only college in the north-eastern region of the country to have this distinction till date.

St. Mary's College

St. Mary's College, Shillong, was opened by the Catholic society of nuns, namely, the Sisters of Our Lady of the Missions (Religious Notre Dame des Missioners or RNDM in French). The college was founded in 1936 by Mother St. M. Aime, provincial superior of the society, and Mother M. St. Rudolph, the first principal of the college. St. Mary's College started with the IA and BA courses, side by side with bachelor of teaching and Licentiate of teaching courses. The training section was opened in response to the requests made by the women of the region to the sisters of St. Mary's Convent, Shillong, to start a women's bachelor of teaching/licentiate of teaching college in the north-east. For a long time, it remained the only training college for women in the entire region. Lady Reid carried the official opening of the college on 25th October 1937. Initially the college started as an arts college; the science stream was starts in 1967, and then the bachelor of home science (B. H. Sc.) course was started in 1975. The College served under 3 different universities – Calcutta, (1937-48), Guahati, (1948-73) and the NEHU,

Shillong from 1973. A UGC- sponsored vocational course on clinical nutrition and dietetics was introduced and the subject is affiliated to the NEHU as a major subject for degree science students with effect from 2001. Under NEHU, the professional B. T. course was change to B.Ed. in 1976 as per NCTE, a national statutory body of teacher education (National Council for Teacher Education) norms. The NCTE also required that all B. Ed. college should be independent institutions with their own campuses and principal. Accordingly, the St. Mary's College was bifurcated in 1999. The B.Ed. section is henceforth to be known as the St. Mary's College for Teacher Education, in its own campus.

Shillong College

Shillong College, established in 1956 as co- educational institution by a body of educationists in Shillong. Shillong College is the second college of the present state of Meghalaya to be run by a public body, as may be distinguished from religious bodies or the government, the first being the Lady Keane College. Affiliation to Guahati University was granted in 1962 and subsequently to the NEHU when the university came into being in 1973. In 1958 itself the college started off with arts and commerce stream classes and the science stream was in 1964. Computer as a study subject has already been introduced and the college authorities are presently exploring the possibilities of opening employment-oriented courses in the near future. The early staff of the college have fond memories of it as having a cosmopolitan air. The college, which began with only night classes then, was a merging ground of students and teachers from various parts of the region. The achievements recorded by the Shillong College are exceptional for an institution run by the public body.

Sankardev College

Sankardev College was founded on 2nd September, 1962 by Srimanta Shankardev Cultural Centre, Shillong, in its own premises. It was first affiliated to the Guahati University and to the NEHU from 1973. The college began with just three students and 6 part-time teachers in the library building of the Srimanta Sankardev Cultural Centre where it continued to function up to 1966. Initially there were only night classes. Later it was shifted to its own building in which it is functioning now. The aim of the founders was to propagate culture, religion and education in accordance with the philosophy of Sankardev. In order to fulfil this objective, the college was later registered as a society under the Societies Registeration Act. As a co-educational institution for higher education, the Sankardev College has a broad-based and catholic character. The college offers arts and science streams of education to its students. It may be remembered that the Sankardev College traditionally received students who were denied admission in the other prominent colleges of Shillong. However, the tireless efforts put in by the dedicated teachers of the college always bore fruit and this has really changed the face of the college over the years.

Women's College

Women's College, Shillong, an Education India establishment, is a Linguistic minority institution (Bengali). It came into being in 1984 in order to spread the light of knowledge to the women of India's north-east. Initially the college functioned from the St. Edmund's College campus under the stewardship of the founder-principal, Dr. B. Datta Ray, who envisioned the education of women, especially housewives, working women and those who have discontinued studies for sometime, as the chief purpose of the college. Shifting to the permanent campus at Upper New Colony, Laitumkhrah, Shillong happened in 1990. Courses in the arts stream only are offered in the college for both plus two and at degree level. Permanent affiliation to the NEHU has also been accorded to the college. Women's College was brought under the category of aided colleges by the Government of Meghalaya in 1991 and it has been included in the list of colleges prepared under section 2(f) and 12(b) of the UGC Act, 1956.

5

Impact of Television

The concept “IMPACT” corresponds to the influence of the medium on the cognitive (knowledge) and affective (attitude) behaviour of the target audience (e.g. the students). Evidences are plenty in scholarly literature than an audio – visual medium like TV always exerts significant amount of influence on its audience. Looking from the audience or users’ point of view, it can be said that people learn a great deal from television, and are usually influenced. “Learning” and “Getting influence” are two dimensions of behavioural change; and again the change is assumed to be positive or incremental in nature. Hence, IMPACT connotes a state of change or gain in both cognitive and affected dimensions.

Television is the most pervasive medium of communication in the world today. As the printing press democratised learning in an earlier era, Television has democratised experience in the modern age. It can spread information with lightning speed and impact. Television also infuse viewers with imagery and values in a subtle, almost imperceptible manner. Its corporate personality, it has been rightly said, it split among the glitter of show business, commercial requirements of advertisement and the professional demands of good journalism. Television combines sight, sound, motion and immediacy with the personal involvement of the audience. Television offers what print media and radio cannot, direct witnessing of events as they take place rather than getting a second-hand report.

Television is also an exciting medium. The electronic magic carpet of Television can transport millions of viewers all over the world to the actual scence of action in a trice. It serves as a direct witness to history, dramatically bringing in the sights and sounds of momentous events into millions of homes.

Television has its greatest impact in the coverage of dramatic and emotional events. Television inject a dramatic involvement into the viewer. It has the potential to approach and appeal to the rich as well as the poor, the high and the low, the literate and illiterate, city-dwellers as much as the villagers. No wonders, Television is already being hailed as the most revolutionary and democratising medium of the present day.

Television has also become a whipping boy of the modern society, a convenient scapegoat upon which it can dump some of its frustrations. Critics of Television today are as common as the many nicknames devised to describe it. Television has been said to stand for transcendental vegetation and variously described as the idoit box, the one-eyed monster and a vast wasteland. Television has been accused of being superficial, inoffensive, uninteresting, preoccupied with violence and sex, catering to the neo-literates while avoiding cultural uplift and never realising its full potential as a social instrument. There are many who blame Television for teaching violence and inciting children to imitate criminals. Many fear that because television does not make complex demands on our minds, it can stunt intellectual growth. At the sametime, it takes away the sense of wonder, inherent in joys of growing up and in the process, accelerates childhood.

Some complain of the decadence or escapism of Television and that the medium, in the main, is being used to distract, delude and insulate. Some even suggest that Television is like drug. Habitual viewers are addicted to Television and need their daily fix in order to get along. Still others see Television as history's most effective educators. Such education, they point out, was once available only to the very wealthy who could afford it.

Television has profound impact on our society. It has changed the life styles of the people and has become a major influence in the culture. Unlike printing, which took hundreds of years to influence the culture, television's impact was almost instantaneous. Television has occupied an important position in today's world and therefore, it has make an impact on the individuals and the society. Television, as a technology has changed the complexion and manner of conveying ideas to people.

Explaining the importance of television, Joseph (1996) aptly mentions, "Having earned a niche for itself in ways that are inimitable and unprecedent, TV has worked its ways as an indispensable member of hundreds of millions of families across the world. To say that it merely educates, informs and entertains is an understatement. For in the seven decades since its invention by John Baird, the fascinating minutiae of how the medium works and influences has put it in a class of its own. From an apparently innocuous box it has metamorphased into the protagonist, altering the very character of human transactions and shaping the way human beings think and behave. This has opened a Pandora's box and fulled a stormy debate on the role of television in human society".

Studies have pointed out that perceptions of the television messages, images and ideas shape the entire social system. Television has contribute to breaking the social barriers and inculcation of the scientific temper in the masses. Exposure to media leads to the appreciation of social and cultural ethos.

For any social change to take place flow of information is of prime importance. It increases the understanding of the people regarding the issue and develops common feeling for the need for social change. Information bridges the gap of understanding between the people and helps them to unite for the cause. Television has done this job by contributing to the information explosion. Saxena points out "Today's information explosion has opened the floodgates of knowledge and curiosity. This is being attributed to the vast television exposure. A majority of our people live in remote villages, cut off from, what is known as, modernity. Till date, they led a life submerged in age old conservatism. But now they are able to see and appreciate what is going around, adding to their information gain". (Saxena, G., 1996).

As part of the media, Television is a way of conveying information to the audience. In other words, the audience gets information (whether good or bad) through watching various television programmes and it is a powerful medium of communication. Particularly, the youth are highly influenced by it and they become susceptible to its charm. This is because their identities and attitudes are in the process of evolving and they are more flexible to new trends. Victor Strasburger believes that adolescence in particular and the youth in general are at a stage when one is neither a child nor an adult. It is a stage of confusion and bewilderment for the young person going through it. Issues such as establishing a sense of identity, independence from parents, relationships with peers and asserting one's place in modern society and formulating plans for a career or job continuously weigh on the adolescent's mind (Strasburger, V.C., 1949).

In order to accomplish these tasks, the youth need input and constant guidance from higher authorities. Ideally, this input and guidance should and sometimes, does come, from official sources such as sex and drug education programmes at the School/College or at the University level. However, lack of such opportunities from help centres pressurises young adults to absorb information from their surroundings, particularly the Television. With its abundance of attractive role models, TV provides a vast library of information regarding the adult world and how adults behave.

Statistics reveal that young people spend more time watching Television than doing any other leisure time activity except sleeping and they spend more time watching Television. However, TV lures many young people to unnecessary doings than they should spend on activities such as studies or outdoor games. TV watching is believed to make young people adamant and inflexible, to grow mature earlier than their age, and to waste their time and become lethargic.

Nevertheless in spite of its negative influence, the TV as a medium can be made use as an educational tool, as a means for development of communication and to enhance young people in the process of socialization. The TV's influence on the youth would depend on the kind and the duration of exposure both of which contribute to the kind of experience a viewer undergoes (Surderaj, Victor, 2002). Young people whose parents are from low income level seems to see TV as a source of information and education rather than of entertainment. According to them, the TV has helped them gain wider access to news and information and raised their awareness about their society. Furthermore, news serves as a source of political information as well as a kind of public information. They also learn about some programmes on health matters, social behaviour, dress codes, and proper language from various TV shows. For many, the TV remains an important sources of news, recreation and information. Thus effect of television on the youth cannot be under minded. Its effects are numerous and may be viewed as negative and positive.

There is a school of advocates which maintains that the television is producing undesirable and negative impact on the society. These advocates are of the opinion that the television has lowered the public cultural tastes, increased deliquency, contributed to the general moral deterioration and has suppressed the creativity. On the other hand, the advocates of the opposite school have noted the positive effects of television on society. They are of the opinion that television helps in exposing sin and corruption prevalent in the society and acts as a guardian of free speech. Further it also brings national cultural and political awareness to the millions of people. Moreover, according to these advocates the television provides harmless daily entertainment at a low cost to the masses. Which one of the view points is correct in the sense whether the television has produced positive or the negative effects on the society cannot be decided merely on the basis of impression. Over and above, it is necessary to understand the type of impact, in terms of functional and dysfunctional consequences, the television has produced on the social structure. All this needs to be empirically verified through systematic studies. Therefore, in this study we empirically attempt to understand and analyse the way the Television Programmes have produced an impact on the college students in Shillong.

The social background of the respondents is an important aspect of any social research. It is with the help of the social background that we can better understand the opinion and the view points of the respondents because the view points, the opinions and the attitudes are to a great extend influenced by the social characteristics of the respondents. Therefore, the quality and reliability of the responses can to a large extent be assessed by the social characteristics of the respondents. Karl Mannheim (1936) in this connection has remarked that, "the opinions, statements, proportions and systems of ideas are not taken at their face value but are interpreted in the light of the life situation of the one who expresses them". It is, thus clear that our thinking is conditioned by our social experiences. This view from famous sociologist amply shows the rationale for studying the social background of the respondents in an investigation.

The form of human life is determined by the environment where he lives. In relation to the environment, age has played a very virtual role for the development of personality. An individual acquires experiences through the ages. The distribution of the respondents as per age group are shown in the Table – 5.1 below and (Fig- 5.1).

Table - 5.1
Age Group of the Respondents

Age group	*Frequency*	*Percentage*
18 –20	57	20.57
21 – 23	148	53.42
24 –26	72	25.99
Total	277	99.98

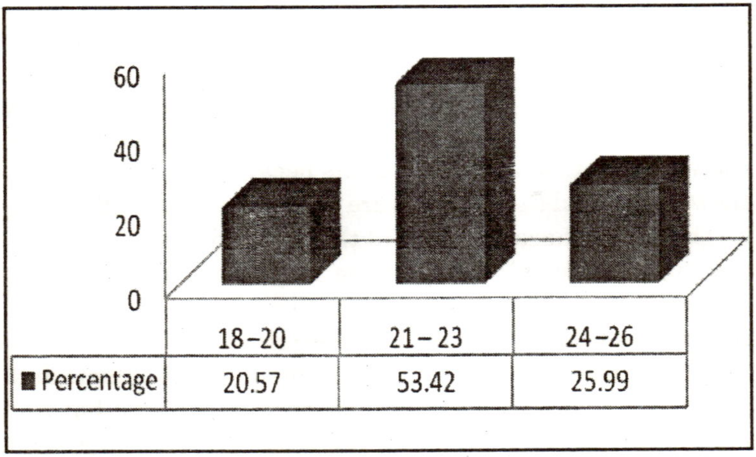

Fig- 5.1 Age Group of the Respondents

Out of the total 277 respondents, the majority of the respondents 148, that is 53.42 percent fall in the age group between 21 – 23, 72 respondents, that is 25.99 percent fall in the age group 24 – 26. Whereas 57 respondents, that is 20.57 percent fall in the age group 18 – 20. Therefore on the basis of the data it can be seen that majority of the college students come from the age group between 21-23.

Table – 5.2
Sex of the Respondents

Sex of the Respondents	*Frequency*	*Percentage*
Male	105	37.90
Female	172	62.09
Total	277	99.99

Regarding the sex composition of the respondents, out of the total 277 respondents 105 that is 37.90 percent are males and 172 that is 62.09 percent are females, Table 5.2. About the marital status of the respondents, it is reported that all the respondents were unmarried.

Table – 5.3
Religious affiliation of the Respondents

Responses	*Frequency*	*Percentage*
Buddhist	05	1.80
Hindu	99	35.74
Seng Khasi	11	3.97
Christian	109	39.35
Jain	03	1.08
Sikh	06	2.16
Muslim	44	15.88
Total	277	99.98

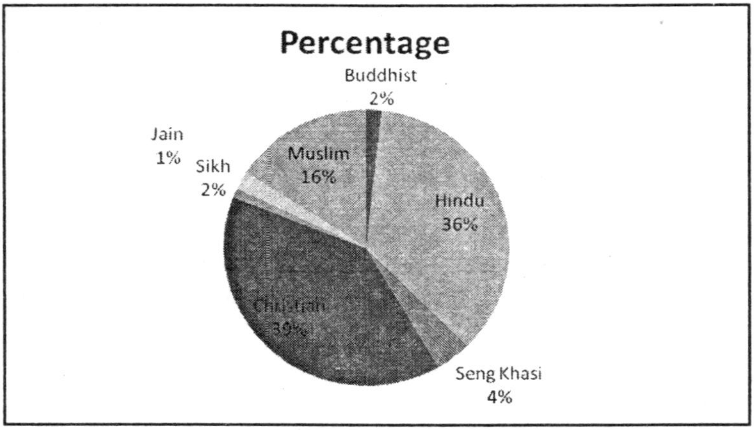

Fig. 5.2: Religious Affiliation of the Respondents

We are living in such an era where we no longer want to believe in any supernatural power. But it cannot be said that the present era has completely avoided the nature of belief in religion. The significant characteristics of the present day life is that on the one hand people denounced the religion and on the other hand man surrender himself to the highest super natural power.

Regarding the religious background of the respondents, as the data in the Table 5.3 clearly shows that majority of the students are Christians that is, 39.35 percent. These includes Catholics, Presbyterians and other denominations as well. Hindus constitute 35.74 percent, which is followed by Muslims 15.88 percent. Seng Khasi, 3.97 percent, Sikh, 2.16 percent, Buddhist 1.80 percent and Jains 1.08 percent. Religions like Seng Khasi, Sikh, Buddhist and Jains constitute a small segment of the percentage from the total which can also be seen from (Fig - 5.2).

Table - 5.4
Birth place of the Respondents

Responses	*Frequency*	*Percentage*
State (Meghalaya)	202	72.92
Other States	75	27.07
Total	277	99.99

It is evident from Table 5.4 that 72.92 percent of the respondents were born in the State of Meghalaya and 27.07 percent reported that they were born in States other than Meghalaya.

In response to the information about whether their place of birth was rural or urban, it is seen that majority of them were born in urban areas (75.09 percent) and the rest (24.90 percent) of them were born in rural areas, Table 5.5 below.

Table - 5.5
Birth place of the Respondents (Rural / Urban)

Responses	*Frequency*	*Percentage*
Rural	69	24.90
Urban	208	75.09
Total	277	99.99

Table 5.6 deals with the data in relation to respondents father's occupation. And it can be seen that 32.12 percent and 29.60 percent of respondents father's reported to be in business and government services. While 14.07 percent of respondents father's occupation were in the teaching profession. In the field of agriculture there are 9.38 percent. The number of engineers of the respondents father's occupation amounts to 6.49 percent. In the profession as doctors accounted for 4.33 percent. Amongst the legal

profession as advocates there were 2.88 percent. Under any other profession which includes pastors, mechanics etc., have been reported by very small section of the respondents which account for 1.08 percent. (Fig. 5.3)

Table - 5.6
Respondents Father's Occupation

Responses	*Frequency*	*Percentage*
Business	89	32.12
Teaching	39	14.07
Agriculture	26	9.38
Govt. Service	82	29.60
Advocates	08	2.88
Engineers	18	6.49
Doctor	12	4.33
Any other (pastors / mechanics) etc	03	1.08
Total	277	99.95

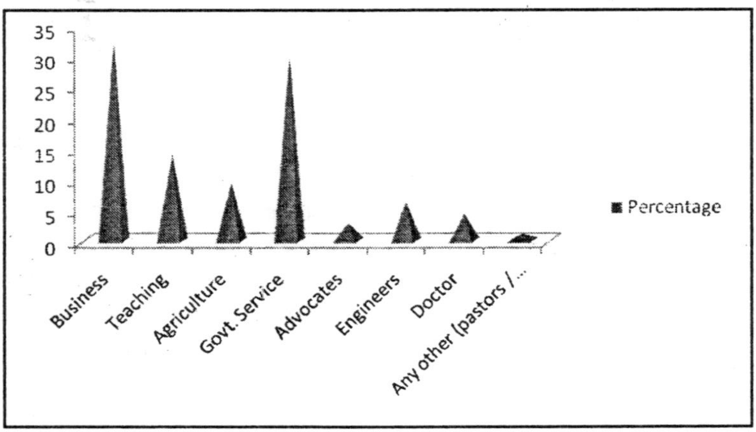

Fig. 5.3 Respondents Father's Occupation

Table - 5.7
Respondents Mother's Occupation

Responses	*Frequency*	*Percentage*
Housewives	210	75.81
Teacher	13	4.69
Business	20	7.22
Govt. Service	32	11.55
Nurse	02	0.72
Total	277	99.99

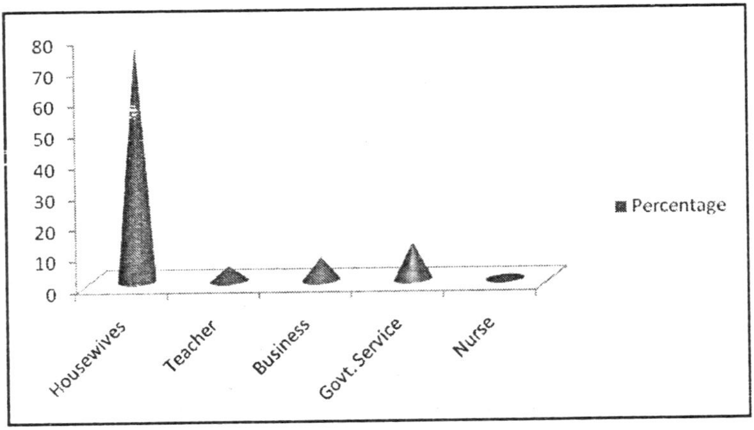

Fig: 5.4 Respondents Mother's occupation

We were also interested to know about the occupation of our respondents mothers'. From the above (table 5.7), it is clear that majority of the respondents mother, i.e., 75.81 percent were reported to be housewives. 11.55 percent of the mother were in government service. While those involved with business were 7.22 percent. As teachers the percentage amounts to 4.69 and 0.72 percent were nurses. (Fig. 5.4).

Table - 5.8
Respondents Stream of Study

Responses	*Frequency*	*Percentage*
Arts	127	45.84
Science	69	24.90
Commerce	81	29.24
Total	277	99.98

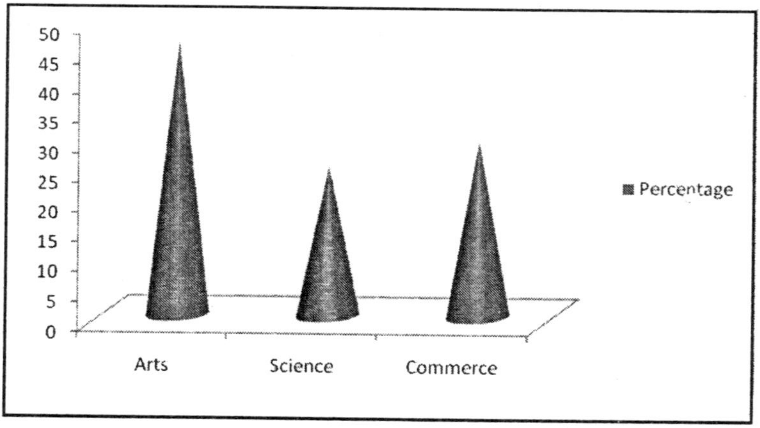

Fig: 5.5 Respondents Stream of Study

The respondents of the present study includes from the three streams, that is Arts, Science and Commerce. From the above Table 5.8 it is evident that majority of respondents that is 45.84 percent were from Arts stream. 29.24 percent of the respondents were from Commerce stream and 24.90 percent were from Science stream (Fig. 5.5)

Table - 5.9
Respondents Class of Study

Responses	*Frequency*	*Percentage*
I Year	87	31.40
II Year	92	33.21
III Year	98	35.37
Total	277	99.98

Regarding the respondents class of study at the Three Year Degree Course (TDC) it can be seen from the above Table 5.9, that 35.37 percent of the respondents were from IIIrd year, which is followed by 33.21 percent of the respondents from IInd year. And another 31.40 percent of the respondents were from Ist year. (Fig. 5.6).

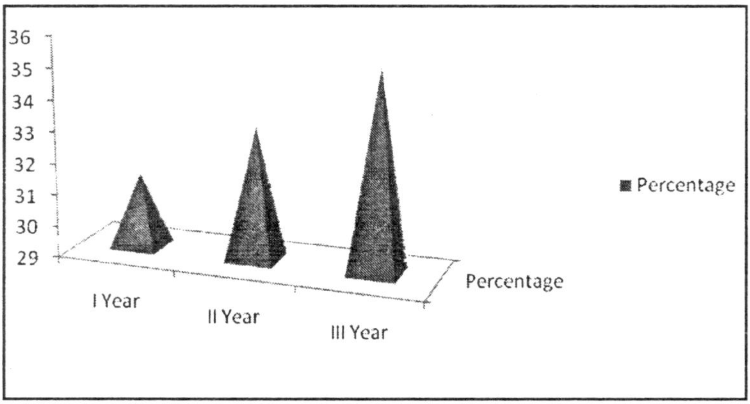

Fig 5.6 Respondents class of Study

Table - 5.10
Spending Leisure Hour

Responses	*Frequency*	*Percentage*
Attending clubs	09	3.24
Games/Sports	21	7.58
Doing Social Works	29	10.46
Visiting friends	56	20.21
Watching TV	119	42.96
Reading Books	37	13.35
Any other	06	2.16
Total	277	99.96

With a view to understand the leisure time activities of the respondents, we enquired as to how they spent their leisure time. From the table (5.10) above it is evident that 42.96 percent preferred watching TV. Visiting their friends has been reported by 20.21 percent, which is followed by reading books 13.35 percent. 10.46 percent likes to do social works. Games and sports accounted for 7.58 percent and attending clubs by another 3.24 percent. Among others which also constitutes 2.16 percent includes gardening, internet surfing etc. (Fig. 5.7).

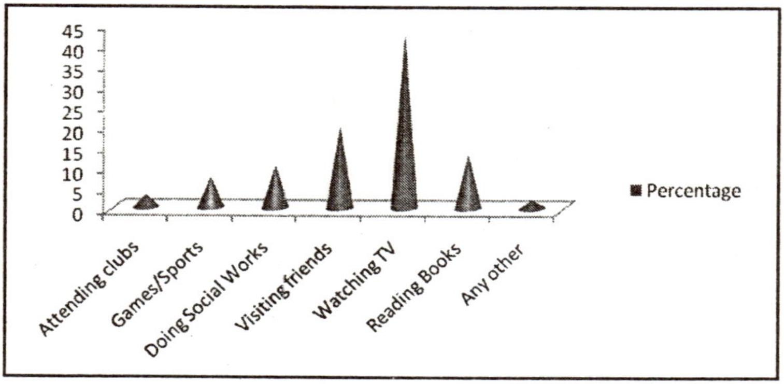

Fig 5.7 Spending Leisure Hours by the Respondents

Table - 5.11
Cable Connection

Responses	*Frequency*	*Percentage*
Yes	258	93.14
No	19	6.85
Total	277	99.99

We were interested to know from our responses whether they have got cable connection or not. From Table (5.11) above it is seen that 93.14 percent of the respondents have got cable connection and only 6.85 percent have reported for not having cable connection.

Patterns of televiewing are the products of the chain of interactions in relation to some common object or goal. They are not an outburst of sentiments at a single point of time. Interactions does not occur in a vaccum. They are shaped and reshaped by socio-cultural environment. The liking or disliking of a person towards a particular object depends upon his attitudes. Psychologists have defined an attitude as a dispositional readiness to respond to certain situations, persons or objects in a consistant manner which has been learned and has become one's typical mode of response. Thus, an attitude represents an individual's or group's more or less stable and observable tendency or predisposition to perform, perceive, thinks and feel in relation to some specific situation, person or object.

Table -5.12
Programme generally watched by the Respondents

Responses	*Frequency*	*Percentage*
Serials	56	20.21
Talk show	08	2.88
News	18	6.49
Games/sports	49	17.68
Musical show	32	11.55
Movies	91	32.85
Animation	03	1.08
Educational programme	20	7.22
Total	277	99.96

From the above analysis (Table 5.12) it is clear about the various programmes which is been generally watched by the respondents on TV. From all the responses, it is evident that 32.85 percent of the respondents generally watch movies on TV. 20.21 percent reported that they watch serials. 17.68 percent like to watch games / sports which is followed by musical shows 11.55 percent. Educational programmes accounted for 7.22 percent. News 6.49 percent, talk shows 2.88 percent and animation 1.08 percent were the other responses (Fig. 5.8).

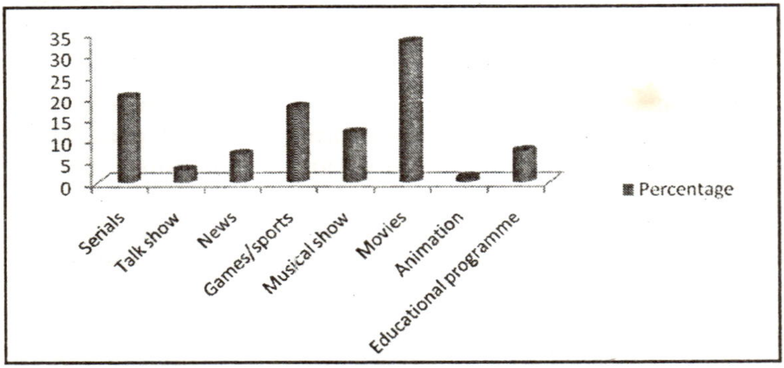

Fig: 5.8 Programmes Generally watched by the Respondents

Table - 5.13
Respondents' interests on watching TV

Responses	*Frequency*	*Percentage*
Story	40	14.44
Actor	20	7.22
Location	09	3.24
Educational Inputs	59	21.29
Places and Things	14	5.05
Fights/Violence	29	10.46
Dresses	35	12.63
Costumes	42	15.16
Cultural Elements	25	9.02
Any other	04	1.44
Total	277	99.95

The respondents were asked to indicate that what they look forward in the TV programmes. To this question it can be seen from the above (table 5.13) that 21.29 percent of the respondents look forward for the educational inputs from the various TV programmes. 15.16 percent of the respondents were interested in costumes. Respondents interested in watching stories accounted for 14.44 percent. Again 12.63 percent of the respondents look forward for dress materials from the various TV programmes. Respondents fond of watching fights/violence accounted for 10.46 percent. There were some respondents who were quite interested in cultural elements which accounted to 9.02 percent. 7.22 percent of the respondents were in the group who interested in watching actors role. 5.05 percent were found interested in watching places and things around the world in various TV programmes, whereas 3.24 percent of the respondents were found interested in location. The remaining 1.44 percent of the respondents were found to be interested in looking other things from the TV programmes like styles etc, which can also be seen from (Fig. 5.9).

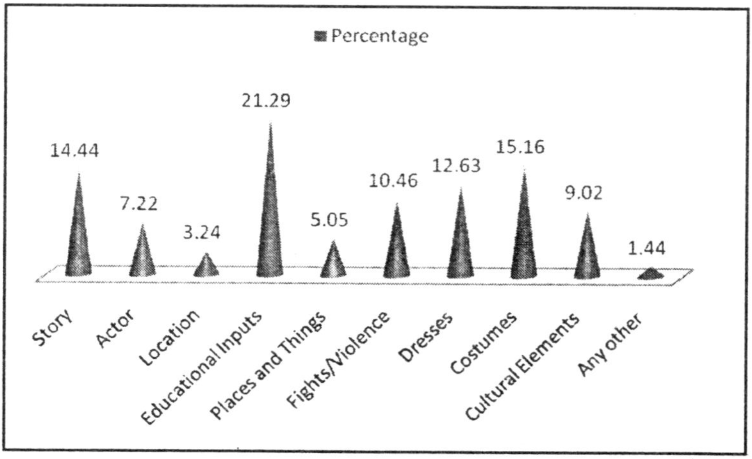

Fig. 5.9 Respondents interests on watching TV

It is well known that most of a person's activity is goal oriented. Need plus goal become motivation for action. Television performs many functions such as providing information, socializing different generations, motivating people for different actions and life styles.

Table -5.14

Television as a means of source by the Respondents

Responses	*Frequency*	*Percentage*
Education	62	22.38
Information	56	20.21
Entertainment	59	21.29
Recreation	31	11.19
Time pass	20	7.22
All of the above	49	17.68
Total	277	99.97

From the above Table 5.14, it is evident that 22.38 percent of the respondents were of the view that they watch TV as a source of education. 21.29 percent watch television programme for entertainment. Whereas to gather information accounted for 20.21 percent. 17.68 percent of the respondents were of the view that they watch television for all the above responses like (education, information, entertainment, recreation and time pass). The remaining respondents watch television either for recreation (11.19 percent) and time pass (7.22 percent) which can also be seen from Fig. 5.10 below.

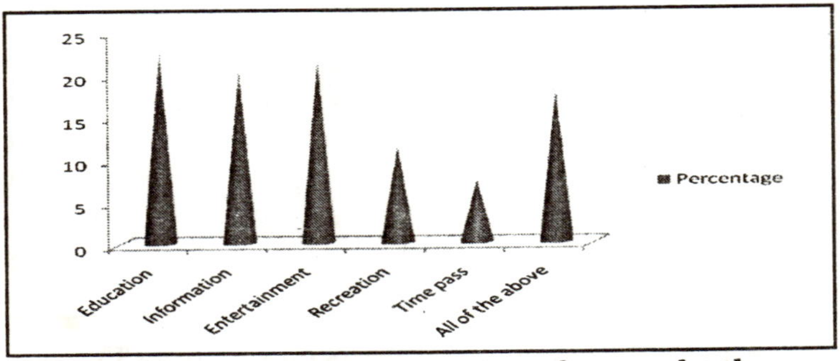

Fig: 5.10 Television as a means of source by the Respondents

Enquiring further from the respondents about their opinion as to what makes them to watch television. In responses we received number of options (Table 5.15) below, where it can be seen that 60.28 percent of the respondents watch television to gain knowledge. 21.66 percent of the respondents accounted that as there is nothing else to do at that time so they watch television. As others are watching television so also 17.32 percent of the respondents watch television. And only 2 respondents out of 277, i.e., 0.72 percent falls under the group for any other reason for watching television other than the above responses.

Table - 5.15
Factors Responsible for Watching TV by the Respondents

Responses	*Frequency*	*Percentage*
Others are watching	48	17.32
There is nothing else to do at that time	60	21.66
To gain knowledge	167	60.28
Any other	02	0.72
Total	277	99.98

It was interesting to know from the respondents about their opinion regarding the telecast of various television programmes. Table 5.16 below is the analysis of the responses about the programmes. 21.66 percent of the respondents feels that programmes on higher studies should be telecast more on television, so that they get the knowledge about various information on higher studies from television, which will help them in their higher / further studies. The other major response where 45 respondents out of total 277 feels that programme on career / guidance and counselling should be telecast more on various television programme which accounted for 16.24 percent. 12.99 percent of the respondents were of the opinion for cultural events. About health programmes was reported by 10.46 percent. 9.38 percent were of the view that television programme should have more of talk shows. The other responses were less than (10 percent) which accounted for current events 6.85 percent, no response 6.49 percent, news events 6.13 percent, documentary films 5.41 percent and reality show 4.33 percent. It can also be seen from Fig. 5.11

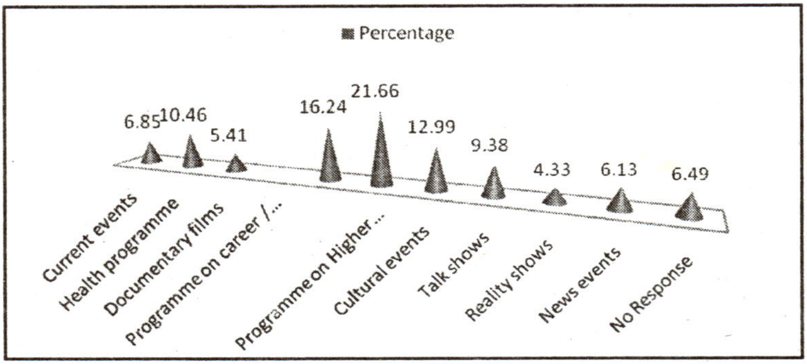

Fig. 5.11 Respondents response on telecast of TV programme

Table - 5.16
Respondents response on telecast of TV Programme

Responses	*Frequency*	*Percentage*
Current events	19	6.85
Health programme	29	10.46
Documentary films	15	5.41
Programme on career / guidance and counselling	45	16.24
Programme on Higher studies	60	21.66
Cultural events	36	12.99
Talk shows	26	9.38
Reality shows	12	4.33
News events	17	6.13
No Response	18	6.49
Total	277	99.94

The languages medium of the television programmes is also very important. Language is the vehicle through which ideas, meanings and emotions are conveyed. It also reflects the barrier on communication of the ideas. It was, therefore, decided to know the preference for the language of the television programme.

It can be seen from the Table 5.17 below regarding the language preference for watching TV programme. To this, it is been found that, 50.18 percent of the respondents prefer to watch programme in Hindi. Preference for English programme of the respondents accounted for 37.90 percent. Less number of respondents that is 11.91 percent have shown preference for regional programme which can also be see from (Fig. 5.12).

Table - 5.17
Language Preference of TV Programme by the Respondents

Responses	Frequency	Percentage
Hindi programme	139	50.18
English programme	105	37.90
Regional programme	33	11.91
Total	277	99.99

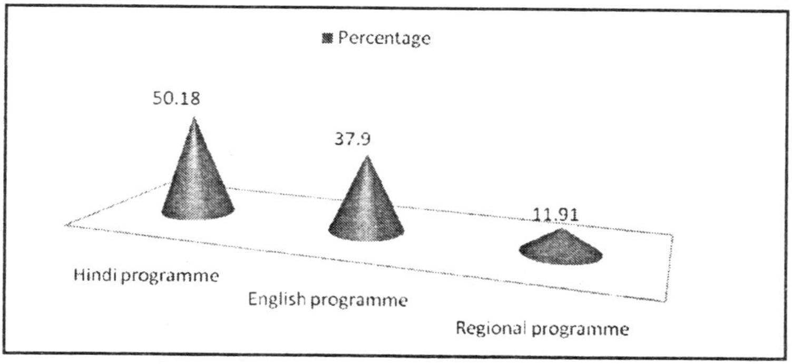

Fig: 5.12 Language preference of TV programme by the Respondents

It was interesting to know from the respondents whether they have the freedom to watch any television channel according to their own wish. To this 73.28 percent of the respondents have responded that they have the freedom to watch any television channel. Whereas 26.71 percent have reported that they do not have the freedom to watch any television channel according to their own wish.

Table - 5.18
Watching Pattern of TV by the Respondents

Responses	*Frequency*	*Percentage*
Yes	44	15.88
No	233	84.11
Total	277	99.99

We were interested to know from the respondents whether they like to watch TV alone or with someone. As regard to this question it can be seen from the above (table 5.18) that 84.11 percent of the respondents do not like to watch TV alone and only 15.88 percent of the respondents like to watch TV alone.

As (84.11percent) of the respondents do not like to watch TV alone, then with whom do they prefer to watch TV were asked to the respondents. From the Table 5.19 below it can be seen that 72.96 percent of the respondents would like or prefer to watch TV amongst their friend circle. 24.46 percent of the respondents prefer to watch TV with family members. And only a small section of 2.57 percent has accounted for any other group, other than friends and family members.

Table - 5.19
Watching of TV by Respondents with preferred group members

Responses	*Frequency (n=233)*	*Percentage*
Family members	57	24.46
Friends	170	72.96
Any other	06	2.57
Total	233	99.99

Table 5.20
Respondents favorite TV Channel

Responses	*Frequency*	*Percentage*
Star Plus	25	9.02
Discovery	12	4.33
Doordarshan	19	6.85
Star World	27	9.74
Sony	13	4.69
News Channel	20	7.22
HBO	09	3.24
Movie Channel	40	14.44
Cartoon Network	07	2.52
Star Gold	17	6.13
ETC	10	3.61
E TV Regional	06	2.16
MTV	29	10.46
Hallmark	13	4.69
National Geography	16	5.77
Zee TV	14	5.05
Total	277	99.92

Regarding the favorite television channel of the respondents it can be seen from the Table 5.20 that 14.44 percent of the respondents have reported for movie channel, which is followed by 10.46 percent for MTV channel. Star World (9.74 percent) and Star Plus (9.02 percent) were the other major response. 7.22 percent of the respondents have reported for News channel as their favorite. For Doordarshan and Star Gold accounted for 6.85 percent and 6.13 percent respectively. 5.77 percent and 5.05 percent of the respondents have said that Zee TV and National Geography were their favourite television channel. Other responses as it is evident from the table accounts for less than 5 percent each, (Hallmark 4.69 percent, Sony 4.69 percent, Discovery 4.33 percent, ETC 3.61 percent, HBO 3.24 percent, Cartoon Network 2.52 percent and ETV Regional 2.16 percent).

An enquiry made from the respondents regarding their preference for watching local TV programmes. To this 75.81 percent of the respondents reported that they do not prefer to watch local TV programmes and only 24.18 percent prefer to watch local TV programmes.

Further an enquiry was made from those respondents who prefer to watch local TV programmes, that what are those programmes they usually watch on the local channel. To this 46.26 percent of the respondents watches local news and 34.32 percent reported that they watch documentaries. 19.40 percent of the respondents watch local musics and dances, which can be seen from (Table 5.21) below:

Table - 5.21

Preference for watching Local programmes by the Respondents

Responses	*Frequency (n=67)*	*Percentage*
Local News	31	46.26
Documentaries	23	34.32
Local music/Dances	13	19.40
Total	67	99.99

With regards to the discussion of the TV programmes watched by the respondents it is found that 71.11 percent discuss the programmes what they watch on the TV and 28.88 percent reported that they do not discuss anything about the programmes they watch.

It was interesting to know from those respondents (i.e., 71.11 percent) who discuss the TV programmes, that with whom do they discuss the TV programme. To this question it was found (Table 5.22) that 43.65 percent of the respondents discusses the TV programmes with their friends, which is followed by classmates 21.31 percent. Discussion with the family members accounted for 19.79 percent and with neighbours 13.70 percent. And only 1.52 percent discuss the programmes with people other than those people as responded by the above viewers.

Table - 5.22
Discussion of TV Programmes by the Respondents

Responses	*Frequency (n=197)*	*Percentage*
Friends	86	43.65
Family members	39	19.79
Neighbours	27	13.70
Classmates	42	21.31
Any other	03	1.52
Total	197	99.97

Allocation of time among various tasks has now become a significant field of investigation for psychologists and sociologists. Time is a scarce commodity available to a person. Moreover, the time is capable of being put to alternative uses. Every person, therefore, makes an attempt to allocate his/her time among different uses in such a way that his/her gratification may be maximised. It is this significance of time allocation which prompted us to know the daily time devoted to televiewing by our respondents.

As regards the daily time allotment of televiewing, it is found that 34.29 percent of the respondents watch television more than 4 hours daily. 28.51 percent devote 3 to 4 hours in watching television which is followed by 15.88 percent for 1 to 2 hours. While 2 to 3 hours and less than an hour accounted for 10.83 percent and 10.46 percent (as shown in Table 5.23 below) and also Fig 5.13.

Table - 5.23

Hours spent on watching TV by the Respondents

Responses	*Frequency*	*Percentage*
1 – 2 Hours	44	15.88
2 – 3 Hours	30	10.83
3 – 4 Hours	79	28.51
More than 4 Hours	95	34.29
Less than 1 Hours	29	10.46
Total	277	99.97

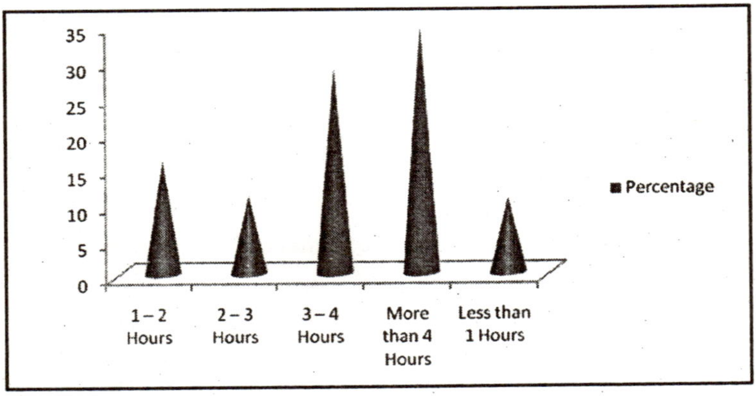

Fig. 5.13 Hours spent on watching TV by the respondents

We were also interested to know from the respondents about their most convenient time to watch TV. As regards to this enquiry 56.67 percent of the respondents reported that their most convenient time to watch TV is at night time. Evening time has been reported by 26.35 percent. 10.46 percent have said that afternoon is their convenient time, and only 6.49 percent of the respondents feels that their convenient time to watch TV is at the day time (Table 5.24 & Fig. 5.14 below).

Table - 5.24
Respondents Convenient Time to watch TV

Responses	*Frequency*	*Percentage*
Day Time	18	6.49
Afternoon	29	10.46
Evening Time	73	26.35
At Night	157	56.67
Total	277	99.97

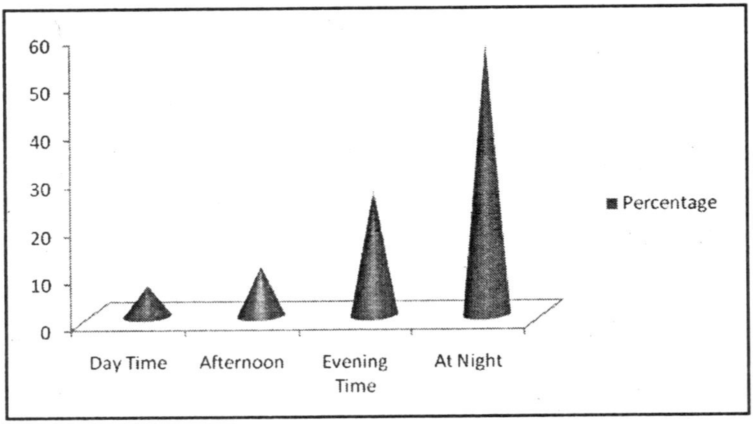

Fig. 5.14 Respondents Convenient Time to watch TV

Next we wanted to know from the respondents whether they are satisfied with the television programmes or not. To this 86.28 percent of the respondents out of total 277 informed that they are satisfied with the television programmes and only 13.71 percent responded that they were not satisfied with the programmes.

Similarly it was interesting to know whether the respondents were tempted to stay on once being watching a programme on TV. The answer to this by the respondents who said Yes accounts for 60.64 percent and 39.35 percent said No.

On being asked that "TV provides entertainment only" out of 277 respondents 71.48 percent do not agree that TV provides only entertainment, while 28.51 percent thinks that TV is the source of entertainment only.

With regard that does TV programme interfere with the respondents study hour, it is been found that 60.28 percent thinks that TV programme affects their study and another 39.71 percent do not feel so, that there is any interference of the TV programme with their study hour.

We were also interested to know from the respondents whether they think that TV programme in Hindi as a medium is a means for a non-Hindi speaking to learn the national language. The response to this is that 50.90 percent of the respondents do not think so, where as 49.09 percent were of the view that TV programmes in Hindi helps in learning the national language for non Hindi speaking section of the people.

Data on does television motivate our respondents to study more, where 89.89 percent were of the view that television motives them to study more, while 10.10 percent have reported that television has nothing to do for motivating them to study more.

As regards how television motivate them to study more, it is quite clear from the (Table 5.25) below that how television inspire our respondents with regards to their studies. 35.74 percent of the respondents feels that by seeing the programmes on higher studies on television motivates them in their studies. 24.89 percent were of the view that programme on competition which is shown on television from time to time help in their studies for preparing them for such competitions in their later life. Another section of the respondents were of the view that by seeing the auto-biography of some great leaders motivate them in their studies which accounted for 21.28 percent. 15.66 percent of the respondents gets the motivation from the television programmes from the various research activities which is shown on the television. And only 2.40 percent have given no response, that how television motivate them to study more.

Table - 5.25
Respondents view how TV motivates them to study more

Responses	*Frequency (n=249)*	*Percentage*
Programmes on Higher studies	89	35.74
Various competition programme	62	24.89
Auto Biography of great Leaders	53	21.28
Research activities	39	15.66
No response	06	2.40
Total	249	99.97

We were also interested to know from the respondents whether they resist from watching television during their examination time. The Table 5.26 gives the picture of the respondents opinion to this question. 35.74 percent of the respondents never resist from watching television during their examination time. 26.35 percent have reported that sometime they resist from watching television during their examination time but not always which is followed by 18.41 percent of the respondents who have said that it depends on their mood. According to the types of the television programmes they resist to watch television at the time of their examination accounted for 15.16 percent. And only 4.33 percent have reported that they always resist from watching television during their examination time.

Table - 5.26
Watching pattern of TV Programmes by the Respondents during their examination time

Responses	*Frequency*	*Percentage*
Depends on the mood	51	18.41
Sometimes	73	26.35
Always	12	4.33
Never	99	35.74
According to the types of programmes	42	15.16
Total	277	99.99

Indian Culture emphasised a great deal on sharing and tolerance. The challenges of modernity of traditional culture are multi-dimensional. Yogendra Singh (1996) asserts that the cultural changes in India mirror both forces of resilience and transformation and that modernization has contributed not only to India's development, but also to its under development. He observes that the quest for economic and social modernisation has activated cultural forces which legitimize values like acquisitiveness, opportunistic utilitarianism, revivalism, communalism and primordialism.

G.C. Pande (1994) however, argues that even if the evolution of modern materialistic culture is parallel with the decline to the influence of religion, the underlying moral values did not disappear altogether. Certain values like love, pity and truth are as much modern as ancient.

Several of the traits that characterize Indian society show uniformity at a certain level of aggregation and beyond that point one sees ambivalence which is at once dichotomous and divergent. Society in India is undergoing transformation due to the cumulative impact of social and economic distortions caused by misinterpretation of religious belief, colonialism, freedom movement and the crystallization of a new normative framework in the form of the constitution and the economic planning process that followed.

By keeping this view empirically we enquired from the respondents whether they think that TV programme distort Indian culture. Out of total 277 respondents 187 respondents were of the view that they agree TV programme distort Indian culture, which accounted for 67.50 percent. And only 32.49 percent were not of the view that TV programme distort Indian culture.

We further enquired from those respondents who thinks that TV programme distort Indian Culture as in what ways. To this 66.31 percent of the respondents were of the view of sex scene that comes on the TV programme and 33.68 percent were of the view of violence/vulgarity which is shown on the TV.

Thus the respondents have expressed the view that the TV programmes are by and large very disproportionately promoting sexism and immodesty whereas in Indian culture chastity, sanctity and secrecy of sex have all along been the cherished ideals. Its public display has not at all been the ideal of Indian culture. Moreover, there is tabooed relations, i.e., relations with whom sexual contact is a taboo. Several of the TV programmes violate these sexual norms of the Indian society.

Most of the TV programmes present very crude and prolonged scenes of violence. The viewers especially youngsters derive hedonistic pleasure out of the combat scenes. The fighters, decoits, robbers and the gang leaders of the underworld beat, torture, exploit, intimidate, demoralise their victims in horrifying and unimaginably disgusting visual presentations. Such scenes arouse hatred, passion, barbaric mentality in the viewers.

Television has the potential for regular viewing and thus in the long run to cultivate the values and beliefs represented by the characters, situation, themes and topics emphasised recently, and thus give shape to the world view on which behaviour is based, as well as for the usually compelling portrayal to affect immediate behaviour among teenagers and adults.

Thus we were interested to know from the respondents that by watching TV whether their mental horizon becomes broaden or not. To this, 236 respondents (85.19 percent) thinks that TV helps them to broaden their mental horizon by seeing the various programmes. 14.80 percent do not agree that by seeing TV programme their mental horizon becomes broaden.

Television has become a reality for many people. Often it depicts a reality which fails to mirror society or life for what it is. Television can confuse people, particularly in believing that what they see on television is the real and complete truth.

To examine whether the changing styles and trends to update oneself from the TV programme as the best medium we enquired from the respondents. 96.02 percent of the responses received was that TV is the best medium to update oneself about changing styles and trends. 3.97 percent of the respondents commented that they do not think that TV is the best medium to update oneself about changing styles and trends.

Does TV viewing affects mindset/thought process was also enquired from the respondents and it was found that 56.31 percent of the respondents do not think that television viewing affects their mindset/thought process. While 43.68 percent thinks that TV viewing did affects their mindset/thought process.

Data on whether Television have any influence on our respondents personal life where it is seen that 60.28 percent admitted that by watching television programme they have no influence to change their personal life. Whereas 39.71 percent have admitted that television have an influence on their personal life.

Television programmes are inflicting crude blows to the family and social values and the structure of the Indian culture. The children and youth are not only receiving confused and faulty socialization but they are also receiving the basest, the meanest and the most instinctive stimuli from the television. Culture stands for the necessities of life – the light and beauty as poet Arnold has put it, but the type of culture the television is projecting is shockingly, debased.

Thus, it lead us to enquire from the respondents whether television programmes inflicting crude blows to the family and social values of Indian culture. Were it can be seen that 84.11 percent of the respondents disagree to this view and only 15.88 percent have reported that they agree to this view.

The distinctiveness of Indian culture, as a matter of fact, lies in the elaborate structure of value based norms relating to the interrelationships in the family, in the community and in other spheres or institutions in the society.

On this the respondents were asked whether the programmes on television, shows the expected social duty towards the family and the community. The answer to this what we have received is that 64.62 percent of the respondents admitted that television programmes show the expected social duty towards the family and the community. On the other hand 35.37 percent of the respondents were not willing to admit that television programmes, shows the expected social duty towards the family and community.

Further we have enquired from the respondents whether television programmes were adequate for them to learn how to respect their elder/ taking care of their old parents. And it is evident that (188 respondents) out of total 277, i.e., 67.87 percent thinks that television programmes were not adequate for them to learn how to respect elders and taking care of their old parents. Whereas 32.12 percent of the respondents were of the view that television programmes were adequate for them to learn how to respect their elders and taking care of their old parents.

Television programmes have mostly emanated from the western soil where contractual societies are the order of the day. There are neither emotional bonds not lingering bonds of friendship or compassion. The Indian culture stands for not only long bonds but also those sanctified by religion, spirituality, morality and ideals.

The cultural crises has been engineered by the Television in India – particularly by the foreign and private channels – and as the new millennium dawns, a cultural holocaust seems to be confronting the nation.

Similarly, we were eager to know from the respondents whether television programmes brings a conflict with their value system, as Indian values and social norms are different from western values and norms. The response to this was that 74.36 percent of the respondents do not agree that by watching television programmes brings conflict with their value system. Another section of respondents i.e., 25.63 percent do agree with the above view.

We also tried to find out from the respondents that does watching television affect family relationship. Where 88.44 percent of the respondents have responded that by watching television it does not affect their family relationship. But 11.55 percent do agree that by watching television family relationship is affected.

For this present study we were also interested to find out from the respondents whether television programmes reinforce the value of democracy, freedom, social equality etc., where 52.70 percent of the respondents admitted that they agree to this view. While the respondents who disagree to this view accounted for 47.29 percent.

Further an enquiry was made from the respondents whether the TV programmes brings any harm than good to their social/cultural life. To this 71.48 percent of the respondents do not think so and 28.51 percent admitted that TV is doing more harm than good to their social/cultural life.

Enquiring about whether the rate of crime is increased due to various TV programmes from the respondents. It is found that 93.86 percent felt that the crime rate is increasing day by day and TV is responsible to some extent for the rise of various crimes like robbery, rape, theft, murder, extortion etc. And only a small section 6.13 percent of the respondents do not think so that TV programmes is responsible for the increase in crime rate.

It was interesting to know from the respondents whether they were by any means influenced by the TV programmes on smoking and alcoholic habit. And the response we have received was that 88.80 percent of the respondents were not influenced by the TV programmes on smoking and alcoholic habits, while only a small section has responded (11.19 percent) that they do get influenced by TV programme on smoking and alcoholic habit.

As the world is changing very fast today, so we were also interested to know from the respondents whether TV programmes helps them to change fast with the world. The response was that 60.64 percent of the respondents feel that TV helps them to change fast with the changing world. And only 39.35 percent of the respondents do not agree that TV help them to change fast with the changing world.

Analysis about the health programmes which comes on television 67.87 percent of the respondents replied that they have gained knowledge about health and fitness from the various health programme from television. On the other hand 32.12 percent replied that they do not gain any knowledge regarding health and fitness from the television programmes. Thus, majority of the respondents were of the view that television have influenced them to change their outlook towards health and fitness.

It was interesting to know from the respondents that does in any way television exposure bring any change in their personality. To this 57.40 percent of the respondents have reported that television programmes have brought some changes in their personality. And another 42.59 percent of the respondents have reported that television exposure did not bring any change in their personality.

Our curiosity was also to know from those respondents that in what ways television exposure brought some changes in their personality which have been admitted by (57.40 percent) of the respondents. The response to this was that 41.50 percent of the respondents have admitted for attitudes. 23.27 percent have said for aggressive nature, which is followed by ideas 22.64 percent. And values have been accounted for 12.57 percent of the respondents.

Violence is on increase in everyday life. The front page of morning newspapers is full of stories of violence by the miscreants, criminals, terrorists, communal fanatic, feudal interest mongers, and by cruel and greedy dowry seekers. Majority of the films today are based on criminal and political themes full of violence and bloodshed. The same are exhibited on television also. The films are usually criticized of being blood stained. Is this true for television also? If so, whether it helps in increasing tendency towards violent behaviour? Here again, our quest is to know whether television is an instrument for enhancing respect for human life and resolution of conflict by peaceful means or, on the contrary, it increases the violent tendencies.

Most of the television programmes present very crude and prolonged scenes of violence. The viewers especially youngsters derive hedonistic pleasure out of the combat scenes which arouse hatred, passion and a barbaric mentality in the viewers. Several of the popular serials have been found to depict vicarious pleasure through violence. Programmes on youth and education (compuses) focus on college-going youth indulging in anything and everything except education.

Our query to this from the respondents shows that 68.23 percent of them agree that the television programmes increases the incidence of very crude and prolonged scene of violence, whereas, the remaining 31.76 percent of the respondents shows disagreement to this view.

Our curiosity was also to know from the respondents that does television programmes will help them in mate selection. As regards to this query it is being found that 75.81 percent of the respondents will not get any help in their mate selection by watching television programmes. Whereas, 24.18 percent thinks that by watching television programmes will help them to some extent in selecting their mate/life partner.

Television is said to be an instrument for increasing lust for romantic life. Films, songs and serials with western pop music all add elements of romance in life styles. By providing a forum principally through entertaining and educating programmes as well as advertisements, TV is said to be creating new strata, affecting the life styles of the people.

Thus, we enquired from the respondents that in any way does television programme influence them to go for pre-marital relationship. To this query it was found that 86.28 percent of the respondents do not get any influence by the television programmes to go for pre-marital relationship. The other response that accounted for 13.71 percent feel that at time some television programmes insist them to go for pre-marital relationship.

It was also interesting to know from the respondents that in any way does television programmes reveal that visit to restaurants, hotels has become a status symbols which is shown in almost all serials and films. On the basis of the data for this enquiry what we have received was that 61.01 percent of the respondents do not agree that various television programmes insist them to visit restaurants and hotels to get the status symbols as shown on the television. Another 38.98 percent of the respondents admitted that, they do feel visit to restaurants and hotels help them to have a better status as shown on the various television programmes.

As the present study is conducted among the college students, so it was interesting to know from respondents whether they were in favour with the advertisement on the use of contraceptives and family planning which comes on television. The response to this query from the respondents was that 55.23 percent were in the favour of such advertisements as they think that these advertisements help to check the population growth. 44.76 percent have admitted that they were not in the favour of such advertisements. They felt uncomfortable watching such advertisement and scenes along with the younger and elder family members. They also felt that the exposure to such acts and scenes is not advisable.

Television programmes, especially serials seem to be bent upon demolishing all the behavioural norms relating to the different social actors in society. One of the purposes of television is to provide entertainment and to make people enjoy themselves. Watching television is a major source of pleasure for many people. Some or several of them may want to experience through watching what others do in public what they privately want to do but are unwilling or unable to do due to one reason or the other, including a feeling of shame or risk of exposure caused by the prevailing social norms.

When we enquired from the respondents that do they agree for some of the theme of television serials is wrong, immoral and against our traditional norms and practices. And it was found that 75.09 percent of the respondents admitted that they were not of the view that serials which is shown on television was against the traditional norms and practices. While 24.90 percent of the respondents were in the view that some serials shown on television is against the traditional norms and practices.

Much of what is shown as social drama and family entertainment on television as serials against the very ethos of Indian culture which is based on peaceful living, cordiality, resolution of conflicts by consultation and intervention by elders for maintaining the established norms of the society.

Similarly we were interested to know from the respondents whether television serials seems to tell the youngsters that love, affection and respect for elders do not really matters when it comes to fulfill one's greed for money. The response what we got was that 92.05 percent of the respondents have admitted that they were not in the view of the above query. Another small sections of the respondents which accounted for only 7.94 percent agree to the above query.

Further we have enquired from the respondents whether television serials often exaggerate what is happening and this further encourages men to commit such act. To this enquiry it has been found that 72.56 percent of the respondents admitted that television serials often exaggerate what is happening and this further encourage men to commit such acts. Whereas 27.43 percent of the respondents shows disagreement to this view.

In modern complex society career plays an important role for all the individuals. Thus, it was interesting to know from the respondents of our study, whether television programmes provides enough information on career options. To this 57.03 percent of the respondents thinks that television programme does not provide enough information on career options. But 42.96 percent of the respondents have admitted that television programmes provides enough information on career options

We were also interested to know from the respondents about their attitude towards the sports programme on television. On this query it has been found that (93.86 percent) of the respondents are satisfied with the sports programmes which comes on television. They were also of the view that television create a positive awareness of sports and contributed to the popularity of sports in society. A small section (6.13 percent) of the respondents disagree that television create positive awareness of sports.

Youth is that segment of society that is most fragile – a passage in life when values, habits, ideas and ideals are thrown out of gear. Young people are the most likely victims of mass media abuse. They are infact, the very target of mass-media campaigns. Fortune, May 1994 revealed the starting fact that teenagers and young people between 20 and 25 have the same tastes in all the major cities of the world. Rural

India too is no exception. Multinational life styles are preserved as part of TV and film culture which is now invading the once sacrosanct real on the village social life.

Thus we were interested to know from our respondents that do they agree television progrmmes has a negative influence on the attitudes and behaviour patterns of the youth. So far as the respondents of this study were concerned, a much larger section (77.25 percent) of the respondents were not of the view that television programmes have an negative influence on the attitudes and behaviour patterns of the youth. But a small section (22.74 percent) of the respondents have admitted that television programmes does have negative influence on youth and their behaviour pattern.

Television has became a medium that exploit large – scale society, a society that we know today. Regretfully, the group that are worst affected in watching television are the youth who then become the prime target audience for television producers simply because they are immune to suggestive ideas and behaviours.

This lead us for enquiring from our respondents whether watching television make life more passive than active right from the childhood. And the response to this was that 66.42 percent of the respondents disagree, while 33.57 percent of the respondents agree that by watching television life becomes passive that active. The opinion whether watching television programmes is like an addiction and its effect is similar to a slow poisoning of the mind, was being enquired in the present study. The response to this was that 71.48 percent of the respondents do not think so, where as 28.51 percent have admitted the above query.

The respondents of the presents study were also asked whether they get engrossed in watching television programmes that their works get delayed. And the response was that (57.40 percent) of the respondents disagreed, while (42.59 percent) of the respondents agreed to this query.

Regarding women issue, we enquired from the respondents whether television can be regarded as one of the reason for women emancipation in India. And the response was that (93.50 percent) think that television plays an important role for women emancipation in India. Whereas a very small section i.e., (6.49 percent) of the respondents do not think so.

Usually it is seen on various television programmes like (serials/advertisements) where the chastity and purity of Indian women is wrongly depicted. Thus, it was obvious to enquire from the respondents about their opinion on television programme where chastity and purity of Indian women is concerned. The response to this was that 58.48 percent of the respondents feel that television is one of the source where Indian women are wrongly depicted. And another 41.51 percent of the respondents do not agree, that television programme wrongly depict Indian women.

It was interesting to know further from the respondents that when asked by their parents/guardians to switch off the television, while they were watching their favorite programme what they do. From (Table 5.27) and (Fig. 5.15) it can be seen the number of responses for this query. 33.93 percent of the respondents get annoyed/angry when asked by their parents/guardians to switch off the television. 20.21 percent try to avoid to switch off the television. They listen to their parents/guardians and switch off the television have been reported by 15.16 percent 14.07 percent have said that it depends on their mood and on the programme, which is been followed by 11.91 percent of the respondents who react to it. While 4.69 percent accounts for no response.

Table - 5.27
Respondents opinion on switching off the TV

Responses	*Frequency*	*Percentage*
Switch off	42	15.16
Avoid	56	20.21
Get Annoyed/Angry	94	33.93
Depends on the mood and on the programme	39	14.07
React to it	33	11.91
No Response	13	4.69
Total	277	99.97

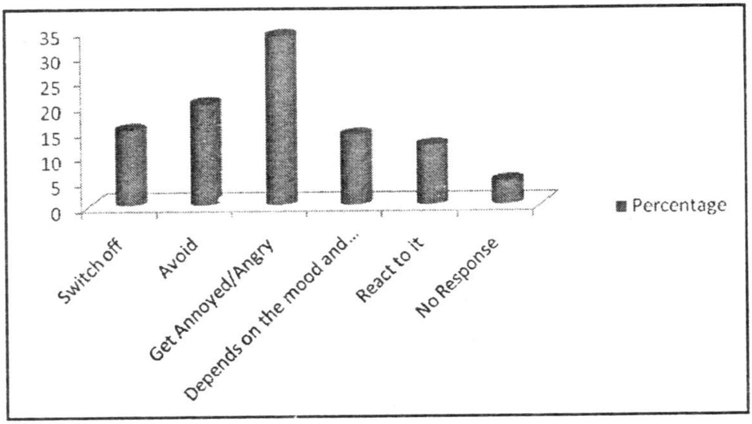

Fig. 5.15 Respondents opinion on switching off the TV

Advertising is one of the functions of mass communication. All productivity relies on this medium of mass communication. Advertising diffuses information about commodities, markets them and persuades the common man of their place in his life. In fact advertising does more than this. It plays a role in social change. It celebrates change and internalizes change for those who become better by using a certain products/

service. In short, advertising is the voice of technology; because of that it represents the intention to affect life. Advertising, though originally used to market products, now, unfortunately, it seems to market feelings, sensations and styles of life; an astounding 'revolution in manners and morals'. All this has been possible through an efficient communication network which has revolutionised changes.

The first impact that one gets from the advertisement is that the viewers have no choice of their own in making preference for the consumer goods they want to use in daily life. The advertisement imposes choices and preferences on the public mind through language, conversation etc. This kind of aggression on the minds of the people, coming from different strata of the society, can create disturbances on traditional way of life of some category of people. In the long run, it is likely that social and cultural transformations of revolutionary nature are created in the society through such programmes (Trivedi, H. R., 1991)

Advertisements are important today, as indicators of social and economic progress. They reveal the direction of change in our values. In fact, a society without advertisements is inconceivable. Advertising has become an important medium of mass education and therefore the role it plays should be taken seriously.

The ever expanding markets for goods and their unchallenged assault through advertisements is flooding the society with information and ideas, attitudes and imagery which is difficult to control and assimilate. This is affecting the young minds to a great extent especially when entertainment is interspersed with commercial messages. Adults may be able to develop a rational resistance to this onslaught, but children may not.

Youths / Individuals are fascinated by TV advertisements. They react to these glamorous, fast paced visuals on TV with their exciting music and their determined sales pitch. TV advertising had entered into daily life of the youths / individuals.

Thus we were interested to know from our respondents whether they are inflicted with the advertisements which are shown in the television. The response to this was that 57.03 percent of the respondents admitted that they are not inflicted by any advertisement which are shown in the television. Whereas 42.96 percent of the respondents have responded that they get inflicted by advertisements from television.

Our further enquiry was from those respondents who have admitted that they were inflicted by television advertisements, which accounted for (42.96 percent) to mention some of the advertisements which inflicted them. From the (Table 5.28 and Fig.5.16) below it is evident that 30.25 percent of the respondents were inflicted by the advertisement of cosmetics. Mobile phones were accounted for 18.48 percent of the respondents. Dress materials have been reported by 16.80 percent, which is followed by Home Appliances like (TV/Refrigerator/Washing Machine/Micro Oven etc) by another 11.76 percent of the respondents. Bikes and cars have been reported by 10.08 percent. Chocolates and soft drinks were the other response which have been accounted for 7.56 percent and 5.04 percent.

Table - 5.28

List of Advertisements that inflict the Respondents

Responses	*Frequency (n=119)*	*Percentage*
Bikes/cars	12	10.08
Mobile phones	22	18.48
Cosmetics	36	30.25
Dress materials	20	16.80
Chocolates	09	7.56
Soft Drinks	06	5.04
Home Appliances(TV/Refrigerator/ Washing Machine/Micro Oven etc)	14	11.76
Total	119	99.97

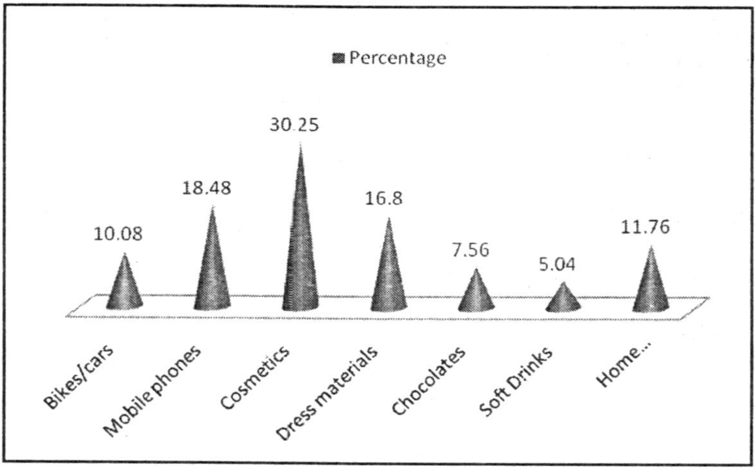

Fig. 5.16. List of Advertisements that inflict the Respondents

Television is the most powerful medium of mass communication in this electronic age. By presenting the news, views, reports and other artifacts in audio-visual form, it has a great potentiality for attracting the audience. It not only attracts them, but it captures their attention also. It is the reason why television is called a glue to the eye. It appeals not to the reason of the viewers, but to their emotions also.

Television has brought the whole world into the bedrooms of the viewers. They need not go to any other place, far or near, in search of recreation, education or information. Television serves their needs in their own bedrooms. Not only this, one can take the service of television, of course, with certain limitations, as regards to their choice, at the time, most convenient to them. Thus the programmes on television strike the man when he is most likely to receive its impact.

Malhan (1988) has emphasized the fact that the social impact of television is recognized as ambivious. It is considered to be from being very good to dangerously negative, depending upon the social propensities of the viewers and their socio-economic backgrounds. According to various researchers, who have gone into these problems, the fault is not that of medium but of what is telecasted over it, that is of the programmes and films which depict titilating bluish situations or scenes of violence or horror.

Thus, our findings on the patterns of televiewing among the college students, we can say that they have farmed a definite attitudes towards television. They have also developed taste for some programmes and distaste for certain others programmes. Television programmes make definite impact on its audience and we have made an attempt to know this impact in terms of the functions and dysfunctions of television as perceived by the college students.

6

Conclusion

Man as a social being cannot help without communicating with others. He had to exchange his ideas and experiences with his near and dear ones. He communicates with others individually as well as in groups through ne or more senses-sight, sound, touch, taste or smell. The modern society has been too complex to function only through direct communication between one individual and other. Most of our important messages must reach many people at a time in order to be effective and meaningful. In a generic sense, media refers to all information of instructional content regardless of the form of storage. Media is define as any form of device or equipment which is normally used to transmit information between persons.

Media that have a widespread coverage are commonly called mass-media, the best examples being television, radio, newspapers and commercial motion pictures. The unscrupulous user of a mass-medium has enormous activity. Mass media work as an instrument for forming public opinion and expanding our national economy through advertising and publicity. They create as well as reflect people's tastes, needs and requirements.

Mass media have contributed to a globalization of our thinking and our relationships. The variety of media and the particular nature of each medium combined with the creative and aesthetic style of presentation make education very simple. It broaden our outlook on life. Media has affected our rhythm of living. Our time tables are adjusted to suit our entertainment time. Thus, it has become a new altar of which we sacrifice money, time, togetherness, social life and values. No aspect of our behaviour, relationships and habits escapes the impact of man-media. Our social conditions, neighbour relations are constantly reported over mass media. Thus, in the age of science and technology importance of mass-media cannot be overestimated. It is felt difficult to spend a single day without the use of mass-media. Different aspects of our lives-social, political, economic and even personal are being influenced by mass-media.

In the 21st century media has assumed a status, which it had never enjoyed before. Starting as an institutionalized approach to generate awareness and inform the masses, media has become an instrument to govern our lives. Rather than a form of cultural expression, it has a culture in itself. With the advent of television and new information technology also came an overall transformation of society-transformation in its thinking, perceptions and expression. No country can afford to ignore information revolution or can resist its all-pervasive impact. The advancement of science and technology has led to an invasion by the electronic media into our lives. The impact has been so great that it has influenced almost all aspects of our lives. More and more youths are attracted to television as a major source of entertainment and spend hours before it. It is not surprising therefore, that it could affect, modulate or control life and behaviour. The urban youths are getting more and more exposed to programmes being transmitted through foreign television channel like BBC, MTV, CNN, STAR TV and others.

Television viewing as it is apparent now days have become a prominent part of the daily life. It has emerged as the most potent and popular communication medium. The double appeal of television because of both audio and the visual media has literally succeeded in keeping people glued to it. Due to its visual effects, sound effects, music, pictures, animation, television is being used as entertainment, information and education media.

Television plays a crucial role in the lives of people particularly the youth and its impact is felt on a large scale. Like other inventions, the television has both positive and negative influence. Although its advantage is felt on the educational, social, political, recreational and cultural aspects; it is not free from certain disadvantages. Today, we see that young people are so caught up by this television 'mania' that their personalities are determined by it. What they see and hear on television has a great influence on them and it has affected their mentality and behaviour.

Inspite of its excessive popularity in the media world, the television gets a bad press for encouraging aggression, violence and romanticizing sex. Television has also hampered family discipline and parental control. Most of the programmes featured on television are exposed to indecent and erotic scenes. The negative impact of television has also affected the education of the youth as they have become so addicted to these programmes that they spend lesser time in academic discipline. The television has also diminished their capacity for creative thinking and imagination. As a result, many of the youth have lost the capacity to wrestle with many burning issues that arises from their everyday life and situations.

On the basis of the empirical research undertaken, out of 277 college students from Shillong, most of the respondents responded to the positive impact of the TV. According to the responses received, 'as a medium of communication and technology, TV plays a vital role in the lives of the respondents and its impact is far-fetches'. The various television programmes influences the minds of the respondents directly or indirectly. In a direct way its influence is felt through spoken words and open gestures and through its indirect means, it employs different messages through subtle or still scenes.

The respondents indicated that the first and the most obvious positive influence of watching television is the increase in knowledge. This is manifested through watching documentary films, talk shows, science programmes as well as the news. Perhaps this goes on well with the common adage that a young person's mind is like a sponge and s/he absorbs information very fast. Thus by watching channels such as the National Geographic channel, the Discovery channel, and even the other less scientific channels, the respondents learn immensely about the world around them, this included both scientific facts as well as non-scientific aspects.

This in turn makes them more conscious of the various cultures existing around them and of other people's customs and traditions. Having learned about the various customs of different cultures, they learn about the uniqueness of every society. Thus they learn to respects people belonging to different cultures and ethnic groups. Consequently, their minds are broadened and this indirectly leads to a greater tolerance of other people and improves the social structure of the community.

The respondents also pointed that apart from the increase in knowledge, TV also raises awareness among them. They are updated with the various events and happenings around the world and is made aware of the realities of life.

The TV is beneficial in developing the emotional aspect of a young person's personality. Various movies, dramas and songs depict the harsh realities as well as the softer side of life. Movies based on true stories and other programmes also open the eyes of the young person and she/he is greatly affected by the various emotional scenes and aspect of the programme. Through these, they are introduced to another aspect of emotional feelings such as suffering, pain, hatred, agony, love, joy, regret, anger, jealousy, happiness, greed, sadness and others.

To reemphasize the advantage of TV, one can say that it does play a major role in shaping the personality of the youth. 'Who they are depends on what they learn and what they learn depends on what they watch.' Of course, we cannot be presumptuous to say that television alone ascertains the personality of the youth. There are other factors like peer groups, parents, and the environment that play an important part in defining the image of the youth.

Despite the fact that TV offers a wealth of information and recreation, its demerits cannot be negated. Television content like human civilization has undergone significant stages of evolution and it first began as an expression of creative thought. Earlier films were on strictly artistic basis where filmmakers would make films that allowed them to express their views on society, culture and human relationships. Through the years, however, TV became a medium that altered perceptions and it wasn't long for producers to realize that TV had a great potential for profit as society evolved into a 'domestic consumer economy.'

Television then became a medium that exploited large-scale society, a society that we know today. Regretfully the group that are worst affected in watching TV are the youth who then become the prime target audience for television producers simply because they are immune to suggestive ideas and behaviours. The question that arises is how far has the TV influenced the behavioural pattern of the youth? Has it affected their life in relation to their parents and other family members? Has it affected their learning and education? Has the TV stifled the youth's space for mental creativity? These are vital issues that cannot be overlooked while analyzing the effects of the television.

According to our respondents, television has been known to cause, or at least is a factor in promoting and encouraging aggression, substance abuse, and immorality. In answer to the question, do you think there are positive values propagated by TV? There was an emphatic No! Perhaps the reason being that TV has projected much of the violence and sex on screen and this has had a negative rebound on the life and behaviour of the youth.

To some extent one can say that there are more of negative than positive values. This has been substantiated in a research done by Centerwall in 1992; where he estimated that ten thousand homicides could be prevented every year if television was less violent.

At another level, television has also taken on the role of teaching adolescent and the youth about sex. In the absence of effective sex education by mature adults in colleges and universities or at home, many of the youth receives all the misconceived information about sex from the TV. This is rather pitiable because television teaches them all the incorrect things about this sensitive subjects and we see its callous nature in the forms of broken homes and disillusioned individuals.

Ironically, most of the sexual references on TV hardly include topic like self-control, abstinence, or responsibility while premarital sex, free lifestyles, living-in before marriage, sex perversion and prostitution are common in primetime shows as well as in movies. It is distressing to note that in the once traditional context like India where sex was regarded as something sacred and 'not being spoken openly', this subject has become over 'familiar' especially in young adults. All these negative influences have been attributed by the TV. The irony lies in that television network forbid advertisements for awareness in pregnancies and sexually transmitted diseases, yet it frequently advertises smoking, tobacco addiction, alcohol and drugs that are responsible for numerous incurable diseases and ultimately death. Although advertising is mostly done passively through logos at sports stadiums or arenas, or in sports cars, the influence on young people is obvious just by observing these over-rated statements.

Interestingly, respondents who are for the negative impact of the TV, points that TV ironically coincides with the increase in teenage suicides and death. In such instances can we say that TV has deviated the psyche of the youth from the normal to the abnormal? The answer is that young people have become more aggressive in their bahaviour which later results in violence. During these past few years in this city Shillong, reports were made that teenagers have murdered, robbed and committed various criminal acts at an alarming rate. Such unlawful acts as these are not confined only to one particular society but throughout where the use of television is extensive.

This project work has attempted to bring out the impact of the television on college students. In a very short span of time, the researcher has made an honest attempt to investigate, analyse and interpret the data collected from the college students between the ages 18 -26 only in the city of Shillong. On the basis of this analysis and interpretation, the project had tried to draw out responses from the questionnaires and summarise the findings of the empirical data in an easy accessible manner. Interestingly, this study has shown that the influence of TV either in the positive or negative aspect has undoubtedly shaped personality development and behaviour on the college students. Although the different concerns of the research undertaken appear to be still rudimentary and the result is heavily dependent upon the students' self-perception. The survey has also revealed that on the whole TV has its own positive points. However, the negative points will show where the intervention of a counselor and parental guidance is needed among the urban youth of Shillong.

Not to blame television for bringing up a grim generation of confused, awry, and irresponsible youths would only be half true. Because it is apparent that television plays a crucial role in the lives of people particularly the youth and its impact is felt on a large scale. Although its advantage is felt on the educational, social, political, recreational and cultural aspect; it is certainly not without any disadvantages. We observe many young people being caught up by this TV 'mania' and consequently their personalities are determined by it. What they see and hear on TV had a great influence on them and it had affected their mentality and behaviour. But the good sign is that of late, there had been a serious concern to protect the youth against the negative influences of TV and various measures have been taken to meet this rising need. Young people are in need of protection not just from commercial exploitation or ideological manipulation by TV but also from the consequences of their own vulnerability and ignorance.

TV as a mass medium performs certain social functions. These include providing information, education, persuasion and entertainment. These days, TV provides more entertainment than education. Added to this woe has been the entry of satellite and cable TV. Now there are more channels of TV and Cable TV programmes than couple of years before. It is estimated beyond doubt that TV watching heavily can have serious consequences such as conditioning of the person to the TV world of reality. This has been the case with heavy viewers of television in the United States. It is proven by almost all the studies that are done, that watching too much of television has negative consequences for the person. A number of research studies conducted on television shows that TV has a negative effect on the audience and it conditions people to believe that TV world is real rather than the real world.

One should learn to watch less of television. This way he or she won't become addicted to TV watching. His or her view of the world will remain normal and the person can lead a normal life. Otherwise, it will become a problem for the person and the society at large.

In India Doordarshan has a major responsibility. It should reduce much of the entertainment programming and give more preference to educational programming. One can learn much from the Doordarshan by this way. Also this will prove harmless to the society at large and to all those concerned with the well being of the society. The Government has also to play a major role in this process. It should reduce much of the entertainment content in TV and impose restrictions on entertainment shown in other forms of satellite and cable television. This will also benefit the viewing public at large. Through legislation and restrain we can bring a change in the functioning of television medium in our country.

Television at present provides more of entertainment than education and information. Today in most of the entertainment programme sex and violence have been added to this medium in a variety to catch the interest of the masses. No one is objecting to the quality entertainment that comes on television, but objection come at times to the programmes which contain violence, sex and negative portray of various sections of the society.

The programme producers of TV in general and Doordarshan in particular should take steps to guard the standards of the programmes that is telecast on Television. 'Television' – miracle of science, if properly used can fulfill all the functions satisfactorily and without 'ifs' and 'buts' it can be considered as a blessing to humanity.

Bibliography

Anuradha, K., 1994, *Television Viewing: Its Effect on Children's Personal and Educational Development*, Discovery Publishing House, New Delhi.

Agrawal, B.C., 1986, "Television studies in India: The State of the Art", paper presented at the International Television Studies Conference, London, UK.

Agrawal, B.C., 1978, *Satellite Instructional Television Experiment: Television Comes to Villages*, Bangalore, ISRO.

Agarwal. Binod C, and Malik, M. R., 1986, *Television in Kheda –A Social Evaluation of SITE*, Concept Publishing, New Delhi.

Ahmad, A., 1980. "Effect of Television study hours of Pakistani Children", *Psychological Abstracts* ***66*** (3), 1414.

Balan, K.R. and Rayudu C.S., 1994, *Effective Communication*, Castle Book, New Delhi.

Beltran, Louis., 1976, "Alien Premises, Objects and Methods in Latin American Communication Research", In Rogers E.M. (Ed) *Communication and Development – Critical Perspective,* CA Sage Publications, New Delhi.

Berlo, David K., 1977, Communication as process: Review and Commentary in Communication Yearbook,1 (Ed) B.D. Ruben International Communication Association.

Berlo, David., 1960, *The Process of Communication*, New York Holt, Rinehart and Winston.

Bhattacharya, Vivek Ranjan.,1976, *Communication in a Global Village*, Chetana Publications, New Delhi.

Bhatia, R., 1997, "A Study of the Influence of TV Advertisements on Adolescents of Baroda City in relation to the selected variables", Dept of HSEC, Faculty of Home Science, MSU,Baroda.

Bhattacharya, R., 1995, "The Indian Family on the TV", *The Indian Journal of Social Work*, LVI (2), April.

Bhattacharya, R., 1995, "The Indian Family on the TV". *The Indian Journal of Social Work*, LVI (2) April.

Brown, R., 1976, *Children and Television*. London: Collier Macmillan.

Bareh, Hamlet., 1987, *The History and Culture of the Khasi People*, Shillong.

Barling, J. & Fullagar, C 1983., "Children's attitudes to Television Advertisements – a factoral perspective", *The Journal of Psychology,* 113, 25.

Bouchalova, M., Bystry, J., Horackova, E. & Vacova, V., 1981, *Psychological Abstracts,* 66 (1), 221.

Breen, M. & Cercoran, F., 1983., "Myth in the television discourse". *Psychological Abstracts,* 69 (1), 319.

Buerkel, R, Nancy, L., Greenberg, B.S., Atkin, C.K. & Neuendorf, K., 1982, "Learning about the family from Television". *Journal of Communication,* 32 (3), 191-201.

Chandrasekar, B.S., 1992, "Doordarshan, Cable and Satellite Television – A Status Report", Paper submitted to International Seminar on Satellite and Cable television, opportunities and challenges, Indian Institute of Mass Communication, New Delhi.

Chaudhuri, M.M., 1986, "India: From SITE to INSAT", *Media in Education and Development*, 19, (3).

Coldevin, G. and Amundsen, C., 1985, "The use of Communication Satellites for Distance Education: A World perspective", *Canadian Journal of Educational Communication*, 14, (1).

Chanda Committee, 1966, *Chanda Committee Report*, Ministry of Information and Broadcasting, Government of India.

Chatterjee, R. K., 1973, *Mass Communication*, National Book Trust, New Delhi.

Chauhan, Kanwar., 2001, *Television and Social Transformation : A study in Mass Communication*, Sarup and Sons, New Delhi.

Chatterji, P.C., 1987, *Broadcasting in India*, Sage Publication, New Delhi.

Census of India – 2001, Series – 18, Meghalaya, part – 2.

Chandra, V., , 2000., *Television and Indian Culture.* New Delhi: Indian Publishers Distributors.

Collins, J., et al., 1983, Television and Secondary School Children. *EMI*, 27 (2).

Chaudhury, S. S., 1994, Teachers' Attitude Towards School Television and its Relationship with Mass Media Behaviour and Job Satisfaction. Media and Technology for Human Resource Development, March.

Comstock, G., 1978, "The impact of Television on American Institutions", *Journal of Communication,* 28 (2), 12-16.

De Fleur, Melvin L and Sandra; Ball-Rokeach, 1982, *Theories of Mass Communication*, Longman, New York.

Danheisser, P., 1975, "The Satellite Instructional Television

Experiment: The Trial Run", *Educational Broadcasting International*, 8, (4).

Dua, M.R., 1979, Programming potential of Indian Television, Communication Publication, New Delhi.

Desai, M.V., 1986, T.V. Input and Impact Social Context and Value System, Mainstream August 24.

Deb, Dipanjali., 2005, A study on Television Viewing and parental control in respect of class – VIII Boys and Girls of Shillong Secondary Schools, B. Ed Dissertation, P.G.T. College, Shillong.

Das Gupta, D. N., 2002, *Communication and Education*, Pointer Publishers, Jaipur.

Dua, M. R. and Gupta, V.S., 1999, *Media and Development*. New Delhi: Har-Anand Publications Pvt, Ltd.

Dua, M. R. and Manonmani, T., 1997, *Communication and Culture: New Perspectives and Applications*. New Delhi: Galgotia.

Dutta, S., 1996, "The Cold Blue Gaze: Television and Power in the Satellite Age". *IIC Journal*.

Eppan, K.E., 1979, "The Cultural Component of SITE", *Journal of Communication*, 29, (4).

Eashwar, L., 1994, "Impact of New Communication Technology on Women as Users and Producers of the Means of Communication", *Media Asia*, Vol, 21, No. 1.

Ganesh, S., 1995, *Lectures on Mass Communication*, Indian Publishers, Delhi.

Gerbner, George., 1956, "Towards a General Model of Communication", *Audio Visual Communication Review* 4.

Gozzi, Raymond D., 1985, "Mass Media in third World: Effects on high context cultures," Published paper Comstu Dept., University of Massachusetts.

Gerbner, George, Larry, Gross, Michel, Morgan., 1980, "The main streaming of America", *Journal of Communication*, 30, Violence profile No. 11.

Government of India, Ministry of Information and Broadcasting, 1966, *Radio and Television: Report of the Commission on Broadcasting and Information Media*, Publication Division, New Delhi.

Gerbner, G., 1970, "Cultural Indicators : The case of violence in Television Drama", *Annals of American Association of Political and Social Science*, 338.

Gantz, Walter and Zohoori, Reza, Ali., 1982, "The Impact of Television Scheldule Changes on Audience viewing Behaviours", *Journalism Quarterly*, Vol. 59 No. 1, Summer.

Ghosh, Subir, 1991. *Mass Media Today*, Profil Publishers, Calcutta.

Gupta, Nilanjana., 1998, *Switching Channels: Ideologies of Television in India*, Oxford University press, Delhi.

Gaddy, G.D., 1986, "Television's impact on high school achievement". *Public Opinion Quarterly*, 50 (3), 340-350.

Gunter, B., 1982, "Does Television interfere with reading development". *Psychological Abstracts*, 69, (1), 84.

Hall, Edward T., 1973, *Hidden Dimensions*, Anchor Doubleday.

Halloram, J.D.E., Phillip and Murdock, G., 1970, *Demonstrations and Communication*, Great Britaing, Penguin.

Healy, J., 1980, Engangered Media: Why Our Children Don't Think. Cleveland: Simon and Schuster.

Jain, G.C., 1978, "Low Cost Television Studio Equipment for Broadcast Applications in Developing Countries", *Educational Broadcasting International*, 11, (1).

Jha, R. C. and Sinha, B.P., T. V. 1980, Broadcast in Delhi: A Retrospective View. IJEE.

Johnson, Wendell., 1951, "The Spoken word and the great unsaid", *Journal of Speech* 37.

Johnson, Lesly., 1984, "The uses of the media : An interpretationof the significance of the mass media in the lives of young people", *Discource*, Vol. 4, No. 2, April.

Joseph, M.K., 1996, Modern Media Communication, Sociology and Communication Revolution, Vol. 1, Anmol publications, New Delhi.

Joshi, Ila., 1991, *Women Dimension on Television*, Concept Publishing, New Delhi.

Joshi, Uma., 1999, *Text Book of Mass Communication and Media*, Anmol Publications, New Delhi.

Joshi, S. R., 1996, "Mass Media and Cultural Identity; Issues of Ethnic co-existence in India". *Asian Journal of Communication.*

Kalra, R. K. and Kalra, A., 1996, "Impact of Cable Television on Adolescents". *Kurushektra*, Jan – Feb.

Katz, Elihu., 1960, "Communication Research and Image of the society: Convergence of two Research Traditions", *American Journal of Sociology* 65, No. 5.

Kent, S., 1985, "The effect of Television viewing : A cross cultural perspective". *Psychological Abstracts,* 72 (7), 2452.

Kincaid, Lawrence D., 1979, The Convergence Model of Communication, East West Center Honolulu.

Kishore, Krishna., 1994, "The Advent of Star T.V. in India", *Media Asia*, Vol, 20. No. 2.

Klapp, Orrin., 1972, *Currents of Unrest*, Holt Rinehart and Winston, New York.

Krishnamoorthy, P.V., 1975, "Learning Through Satellite Broadcasting", *Literacy Discussion*, 6, (3).

Kumar, Narendra and Chandiram., 1967, *Educational Television in India*, Arya Book Depot, New Delhi.

Kunhi Krishnan, K., 1990, "Impact of Television". *The Hindu,* 7th October, 19.

Lasswell, Harold D., 1948, "The structure and Function of Communication in Society", in Bryson Lyman (ed), *The Communication of Ideas*, Harper and Row, New York.

Lowry, Dennis, T., 1981, "Alcohol Consumption patterns and consequences on prime – time Network T.V.", *Journalism Quarterly* vol. 58, No. 1, Spring.

Luthra, H.R., 1986, *Indian Broadcasting*, Publications Division, Ministry of Information and Broadcasting, Government of India, New Delhi.

Lyndem, Biloris, and George, Siby. K., 2003, *Higher Education in Meghalaya : An Analysis for the Future*, DVS Publishers, Guwahati.

Maniar, A., 1994, "Influence of Television Viewing on Adolescents as perceives by themselves and their mothers in relation to selected variables", M.Phil. Dissertation, M.S. University of Baroda, Baroda.

Mann, G.S., 1987, *The Story of Mass Communication*, Harnam Publication, New Delhi.

Maherzi, Lotfi., 1997, *World Communication Report*, UNESCO, Paris.

Markandan, N., . 1996, "Mass Media on the Grass Roots: A Threat or an Opportunity?" *Kurushektra*, Jan - Feb.

Maccoby, E.E. 1951, "Television: Its impact on school children". *Public Opinion Quarterly,* 15, 521-444.

Mahajan, Kamlesh, 1990, *Television and Women's Development*, Classical Publishing, New Delhi.

Mac Bride, Scan., 1980, *Many Voices, one world,* Kogan Page Ltd, London/ Unipub, New Delhi.

McLuhan, Marshall., 1965, *Understanding Media: The Extensions of Man*, McGraw Hills, New York.

McCombs, Maxwell E. and Shaw, Donald L., 1972, "The Agenda Setting Function of the Mass Media", *Public Opinion Quarterly* 36.

Mehra, S., 1985, *Sociology of Television Viewing Behaviour.* Varanasi: NCDC.

Mitra, Ananda., 1993, *Television and Popular Culture in India: A Study of the Mahabharat,* Sage Publication, New Delhi.

Mirchandani, G.C., 1976, *India Backgrounders – Television in India*, Vikrant Press, New Delhi.

Mittal, Sujata., 2005, *Children and Media*, ISHA Books, Delhi.

Mody, B., 1978, "Lessons from the Indian Satellite Experiment", *Educational Broadcasting International*, 11, (3).

Mody, B., 1979, "Programming for SITE", *Journal of Communication*, 29, (4).

Mouly, G.J., 1964, *The Science of Educational Research*, Eurasia Publishing House, New Delhi.

Mohanty, Jagannath., 2003, *Modern Trends in Educational Technology*, Neelkamal Publications, New Delhi.

Mohanty, J., 1984, *Educational Broadcasting: Radio and Television in Education*, Sterling Publishers, New Delhi.

Mulay, V., 1978, "The Teacher in the Sky: Prospects", *Quarterly Review of Education*, 8, (4)

Narula, U., 1986, "New Communication Technologies in Developing Countries: A case of India", The paper presented at the conference organised by the International Association for Mass Communication Research, New Delhi., 25-29 August.

Narula, Uma., 1994, *Mass Communication: Theory and Practice*, Har - Anand Publications, New Delhi.

Narula, Uma., 1993, *Mass Media in India: Four Decades.*

Narayanan, A., 1983, "The Impact of T.V. on Indian Families: A case study of Bombay T.V. Viewers." Ph.D. Thesis, Vadodara : Department of Sociology, University of Baroda.

Narayan, A., 1987, *The Impact of Television of Viewers.* Somaiya Publications Pvt. Ltd. Bombay.

Ninan, S., 1995, *Through the Magic Window: Television and Change in India.* New Delhi: Penguin Books.

Noelle, Neumann, Elizabeth., 1974, "The spiral of silence – A Theory of publication", *Journal of Communication.* 24.

Norwood, F., 1978, "Broadcast Satellite: Appropriate Technology Available Now", *International Educational and Cultural Exchange,* 13, (3).

Prasad, N., , 1995, *A Vision Unveiled – Women on Television.* New Delhi: Har-Anand Publication.

Purushothaman, S., and Stella, Antony., 1998, *Media and Technology in Distance Education,* Indian Publishers, Ambala.

Rahman, S., 1974, "Technology and Communication – An Indian Experience", *ASPBAE Journal,* 9 (1).

Rahim, A., 1994, "Impact of Cable TV on Television and Video Viewing in Hyderabad: A Survey", *Media Asia,* Vol. 21, No. 1.

Raghavan, Jyoti.,2000, "Commercialization of the Media, Vidura", Vol. 37. Issue No. 1.

Rao, Bhaskara, N., 2000, "Media Scene Perspectives", *Vidura*, Vol. 37, Issue No. 1.

Ravindran, R. K., 1999, *Media and Society*. New Delhi: Commonwealth Publishers.

Ribeiro de Almedia, A. & Aparcido da Silva, J., 1982, "Television parents and children : A study of daily preference and habits." *Psychological Abstracts,* 68 (1), 620.

Riju, Jung, S., 1982, "Public Affairs and Sensationalism in Local T.V. News programmes", *Jouranalism Quarterly* Vol. 59, No. 1, Spring.

Rogers, William., 1984, *Communication in Action Holt*, Rinehart and Winston, New York.

Rogers, Everett M., 1986, *Communication Technology: The New Media in Society*, The Frees Press, New York.

Rymbai R. T., 1979, *The Khasi Heritage*, Shillong.

Rubinstein, E.A., 1981, "Book review on : Television and Social Behaviour; Beyond Violence and children." *Harvard Educational Review,* 51 (1), 331.

Saksena, Gopal., 2000, "Forty Years of Television in India", *Vidura*, Jan – Mar, Vol., 37, issue, 1.

Saksena, G., 1996, *Television in India: Changes and Challenges*. New Delhi: Vikas Publishing House, Pvt. Ltd.

Saxena, G., 1996, *Television in India: Changes and Challenges*, Vikas Publishing House, New Delhi.

Schramm, W., 1973, *Men, Message and Mesia – A Look at Human Communication*, Harper and Row publishers, New York. Shannon, C.E and Weaver, W., 1949, *The mathematical Theory of Communication,* Urbana: University of Illinois Press.

Schramm, Wilbur., 1977, *Big Media, Little Media,* California: Institute for Communication Research, Stanford University.

Schramm, W., Lyle, J. & Parker, E., 1961, *Television in the Lives of Our Children,* Standford, Calif: Standard University Press.

Schramm, W.W. & Roberts, D.F., 1971, "Children's learning from the mass media" In : Schramm. W, & Roberts D.F. (Eds.), 1971. *The Process and Effects of Mass Communication,* University of Illinois Press, Urbana, Illinois, 596-611.

Sen, Monideepa., 1988, "Social Aspects of Mass Media: A Study of Television coverage in Meghalaya", M.Phil Dissertation, Department of Sociology, NEHU, Shillong.

Sen Gupta, Surojit., 2006, *Urban Social Structure : A Study of a Hill City,* Akansha Publishing House, New Delhi.

Sen Gupta, Surojit., 2004, Shillong at the turn of 21st century, In Sen Gupta, Sutapa (ed), *Shillong: A Tribal Town in Transition,* Reliance Publishing House, New Delhi.

Sen Gupta, Surojit., 2006, *Role of Television in Society,* The Edmundian, St. Edumund's College, Shillong.

Sharma, B,M., 1994, *Media and Education,* Commonwealth Publishers, New Delhi.

Sharma, Sita Ram., 1996, *Media and World Education* (Vol – 1,2,&3), Sarup and Sons, New Delhi.

Shanon, C.E and Weaver, W., 1949, *The Mathematical Theory of Communication,* Urbana: University of Illinois Press.

Shaw, L Donald, and Combs, Maxwell Mc., 1977, *The Emergence of American Political Issues, The Agenda Setting Function of the Press*, St. Paul Min Weit publishing.

Shukla, S., 1979, "The Impact of SITE on primary school children", *Journal of Communication*, 29, (4).

Sinha, A.C., 1986, *Video penetration in N.E.I. Department of Sociology*, NEHU, Shillong.

Sing, Yogendra., 2005, *Modernization of Indian Tradition*, Rawat Publications , New Delhi.

Singh, R., 1992, "Impact of Television on The Indian Society". *Integration*, X (1).

Singer, J.L. & Singer. D.G., 1986, "Family experiences and television viewing as predictors of children's imagination, restlessness and aggression". *Psychological Abstracts,* 74 (9), 1324.

Skornia, H.J., 1965, *Television and Society – An Inquest and Agenda for Improvement*, McGraw Hills.

Sondhi, K., 1980, *Problems of Communication in Developing Countries*, Vision Books, New Delhi.

Sondhi, Kishen., 1985, *Communication and Values*, Somaiya Publication, Bombay.

Stein, Jay, W., 1979, *Mass Media, Education and a Better Society*, Nelson-Hall, Chicago.

Strasburger, Victor C., 1949, *Adolescents and the Media Medical and Psychological Impact*, Sage Publications, London.

Sudrashan, K,N., and Singh, U.K., 2004, *Media Education*, Discovery Publishing House, New Delhi.

Suria Kanthi, A. & Meenakshi, D., 1989, "Parental views on

the usefulness of television programmes to children", *Experiments in Education,* 17 (7), 174-177.

Tannis, Macbeth Willians., 1986, *The Impact of Television,* Academic Press, INS.

Tan, Alexis, S.and Kinner, Denise., 1982, "TV Role models and anticipated Social Interaction", *Journalism Quarterly* Vol 59, No. 4 Winter.

Tangney, J.P.,1988, "Aspects of the family and children's television viewing content preferences". *Child Development,* 59 ( ), 1070-1079.

Thompson, Denys (ed), *Discrimination and Popular Culture,* G.B, Penguin.

Trivedi, H.R., 1991, *Mass Media and New Horizons,* Concept Publication, New Delhi.

Tucker, L.A., 1986, "The relationship of television viewing to physical fitness and obesity". *Psychological Abstracts,* 74 (5), 1528.

Unnikrishnan, N, and Bajpai, S., 1996, *The Impact of Television Advertising on Children.* New Delhi: Sage.

UNESCO., 1980, *Many Voice – One World,* Kogan Page Ltd, London, in Association with World Association for Christian Communication.

Veith, Richard H., 1983, *Television's Teletext,* North-Holland, New York.

Vidya Sagar, M., 1978, "Bombay TV: imbalance", *Vidura,* 15, 219.

Williams, Fredrich., 1984, *The New Communications,* Belmont, Calif Wordsworth.

Wright, Charles R., 1975, *Mass Communication, A Sociological Perspective,* 2nd (ed), Random House, New York.

Weiner, Norbet., 1950, *The Human use of Human Beings: Cybernetic and Society*, Boston Haughton Mifflin Co.

Wimmer, R. D. and Dominick, J.R., *Mass Media Research: An Introduction*, California: Wadsworth.

Williams, T.M. (Ed), 1980, *The Impact of Television: A Natural Experiment in Three Communities*. New York: Academic Press, Inc.

Vishwanathan, T., 1992, Telecommunication Switching Systems and Networks, Prentice Hall, New Delhi.

Yadav, J.P., 2004, *Television and Social Change*, Vol I, Anmol Publications, New Delhi.

Young, Pauline V., 1996, *Scientific Social Surveys and Research*. New Delhi: Prentice Hall of India.

Zuckerman, D.M. Singer, D.G., & Singer, J.L., 1980, "Television viewing, children's reading and related classroom behaviour". *Journal of Communication*. 30 (1), 166-173.

Index

■■■